SPIDERS
OF THE
WORLD

SPIDERS
OF THE
WORLD

Rod & Ken Preston-Mafham

BLANDFORD

Paperback edition first published in the UK 1993
by Blandford, a Cassell imprint

Cassell plc,
Wellington House
125 Strand
London
WC2R OBB

Reprinted 1994, 1998 & 1999

Previously published in hardback by Blandford in 1984
Reprinted 1985, 1988 & 1989

Text copyright © 1984 & 1993 Rod & Ken Preston-Mafham
Photographs copyright © 1984 & 1993 Premaphotos Wildlife Ltd

The right of Rod & Ken Preston-Mafham to be identified as the authors
of this work has been asserted by them under the provisions of the
UK Copyright, Designs and Patents Act 1988.

Distributed in the United States by
Sterling Publishing Co., Inc.,
387 Park Avenue South, New York, NY 10016–8810

A Cataloguing-in-Publication Data entry for this title is available
from the British Library

ISBN 0–7137–2392–0

Typeset in the UK by August Filmsetting, Haydock, St Helens

Printed and bound by Colorcraft Ltd, Hong Kong

Contents

Preface

Despite the feelings of revulsion inspired in many people by the mere thought of spiders, it is impossible to deny that they are fascinating creatures with a unique and unusual life style. Our interest in spiders has grown and matured over the last 10 years, culminating in the writing of the present volume. As well as being wildlife photographers, we are both very keen conservationists and naturalists in the most general sense and it is in this context that our interest in spiders has developed over the past decade. Initially, we were involved in the collection and identification of spiders in Warwickshire and Gloucestershire, England, particularly in nature reserves, where the spider fauna was mostly virtually unknown, and this work resulted in the addition of a respectable number of new species of spiders to the county lists. At the

Plate 1. A beautiful green jumping spider of the family Salticidae. Australia.

same time we were building up a considerable collection of colour transparencies of British spiders, to be supplemented in more recent years by pictorial coverage of spiders from far-flung parts of the world as our foreign travel increased. Anxious to imbue a greater appreciation of the beauty of spiders in the minds of the general public, we started to give lectures to local societies, talking either on spiders as a main subject or perhaps featuring them prominently in talks based on various terrestrial habitats. At the end of each lecture, we were frequently asked to name a book which could introduce the novice to the subject of spiders in general and it was the lack of such a book that finally led us to write the present volume.

There are, of course, already a number of excellent books about spiders available to the reader and we have included a brief resumé of these in a section on further reading at the back of this book. Most of these, however, are aimed more at the dedicated arachnologist than the general reader, for whom they may be rather hard going, while none of them attempts in a really general way to give the reader a basic introduction to spiders on a worldwide basis. However, all these books should be read at some time by the amateur with any interest at all in spiders and we hope that, having read this book, the reader will have his appetite whetted for further reading on the subject.

Although we have tackled the subject of spiders on a worldwide basis, it has only been possible to scratch the surface in this single volume, since to do justice to the 30 000 known species of spiders in the world would entail years of work, much new research and the writing of a whole library of bulky tomes. What we have done, therefore, is to choose a number of representative spider families, selecting mainly those whose members are most likely to be noticed by the casual observer. From within these families, we have then chosen representative species to give the reader some idea of the great diversity of structure and life styles to be found in spiders. We should perhaps stress that in no way is this book designed to be used as an aid to the identification of individual spiders and books intended for this purpose are named in the section on further reading. The reader may be struck by the almost constant choice of the female spider to illustrate various points throughout the text. This is a deliberate choice and has nothing to do with a kind of reverse male chauvinism for, in spiders, the male is of little significance, except during the mating act, and many male spiders are so small and insignificant that an enormous preponderance of females is usually encountered.

In writing a book for the non-specialist, there is always a problem with biological nomenclature and, since spiders have a number of structures unique to themselves, the use of certain scientific terms within the text has been unavoidable: we have therefore included a comprehensive glossary which we hope will explain any strange words encountered by the reader. The majority of spiders lack common names and we have, therefore, had to resort almost exclusively to their scientific names, whose usage has been explained in the text.

With only a single exception, we have taken all the photographs in this book ourselves and are pleased to be able to assure the reader that they portray the lives of spiders as accurately as possible for, in keeping with our general policy, all the subjects were photographed wild and free in their natural habitat. With persistence, even the most evasive subjects, such as certain tropical jumping spiders, can be photographed in the wild and we have always felt that subduing spiders or any other animals and then photographing them in an artificial setting tends to give artificial results. In our selection of pictures, we have tried to illustrate as many examples of spider behaviour as possible, while at the same time maximising the number of species chosen. In certain cases, however, we felt it wise to select a single common species to illustrate various aspects of a single spider life history.

In travelling around the world, taking a broad coverage of wildlife pictures, it is inevitable that we have been helped by numerous generous people and we give them all our thanks. With specific reference to our work on spiders, we are particularly grateful to Dr John Cooke and to John and Francis Murphy for help in identifications. We would also like to thank Jean Preston-Mafham for all her help and encouragement, and for the work she has put into the production of the index. Our final thanks go to Paula Chasty for the excellent job she has done in producing all of the line drawings used in the text.

Rod and Ken Preston-Mafham
King's Coughton, 1983

9

Chapter 1
Introduction to Spiders

Currently, about 30 000 species of spiders have been recognised, although it is certain that many more have yet to be discovered from all parts of the world. The spiders are known to occupy nearly every terrestrial habitat, from the peaks of the highest mountain ranges to the depths of the largest caves and pot-holes, from damp marsh to dry desert, anywhere in fact that they can find other arthropods to provide them with a meal. Some spend at least part of their lives running around on the surface of freshwater lakes and ponds and a few of these can dive to safety and survive below the surface of the water for a short time, although only the true water spider, *Argyroneta*, has perfected this ability to the extent that it is able to live a wholly aquatic existence. A few spiders live along the coastal strandline and some of them can tolerate immersion in salt water while the tide is in.

Although many species of spiders have a fairly wide distribution both within and between the continents of the world, the majority tend to be found within a fairly restricted habitat because they are specifically adapted to live in that particular area. A spider adapted for living in a damp, marshy habitat, for example, would find it impossible to live in the hot, dry conditions met within deserts. Such a habitat preference is well illustrated in two very closely related jumping spiders of the genus *Salticus*. *Salticus scenicus* (Plate 1.1) is the very common black and white zebra spider, found in both Europe and North America, normally on the outside of buildings and on stone walls around human habitations, although it also occurs amongst

Plate 1.1. *Salticus scenicus*. This jumping spider, commonly called the zebra spider, seen here sitting on a cultivated cactus, illustrates the way in which members of this family gaze at a human being (in this case the photographer) using their large pair of front eyes. Europe and USA.

rocks in more natural situations. *Salticus cingulatus* is almost indistinguishable from its relation, at least to the inexperienced eye, and in its European range it is usually found on tree trunks, posts, or gates in or near woods and is never found in the situations occupied by the zebra spider. Despite their similarity, therefore, each of these species is in some way specially adapted to live in its own limited habitat. The zebra spider is only one of a fairly large number of spiders found on both sides of the Atlantic, some occurring naturally, others having been introduced by man as he and his goods and chattels have moved from Europe to the New World. Similar examples of spiders being distributed by man will be met with later in the text for, inadvertently or otherwise, it has happened on many occasions.

All spiders are carnivorous and feed almost exclusively upon prey which they have caught for themselves, although a few species take advantage of food which has been taken by other spiders and one family feeds exclusively upon other spiders. They prey upon other arthropods, mainly insects, although woodlice and centipedes may also be taken, but, as many people are probably aware, some of the larger mygalomorph spiders, e.g. the so-called bird-eating spiders and their kin, are able to consume small vertebrates, including the occasional bird, when they can catch them. It is the large numbers of insects, many of them pests, that are trapped by spiders that make them invaluable to man and to the balance of nature in general and it is almost certainly true to say that spiders catch and eat more insects than all of the other insectivorous animals put together. When one considers that, at certain times of the year, there may be as many as 2 million spiders in an acre of undisturbed English grassland, each of which, under ideal conditions, may take one small insect per day, then some idea of their prey-catching powers may be appreciated. Add to this the large numbers of small insects, such as aphids, which become trapped in the webs of large spiders but are not used by them as food, then the numbers destroyed are even greater.

Despite this enormous benefit of spiders to members of the human race, man's attitude towards them remains highly ambivalent. To the inhabitants of warmer countries, where lack of doors and windows may make the entry of spiders into human habitations relatively easy, such visitors are accepted as part of everyday life and they may indeed be welcome, since their depredations upon less welcome inmates, such as cockroaches, may be very much appreciated. In many countries, especially the USA and Australia, the inhabitants have to learn to live alongside some of the more dangerous, poisonous species, such as the black widow and funnel web spiders. It is very surprising, therefore, to find that, in the British Isles, where all of the resident spider species are harmless, many people hold them in great dread and it is not only the fair sex to whom this applies, since there are plenty of men who are quite perturbed at finding a large, hairy but completely harmless house spider (Fig. 1.1) in the bath. One point which does need clearing up at this juncture is how the spiders arrive in the bath in the first place. It is, in fact, a

Fig. 1.1. *Tegenaria gigantea.* The common European and American house spider running across a carpet; the large body and relatively short legs are characteristic of the female.

myth that the house spider comes up the plughole, as species of *Tegenaria* are not aquatic and very quickly drown in water. What one usually finds in the bath is the long-legged male, who, having reached maturity, has left his web and gone in search of a female in her web. If, during his search, the hapless male falls into the bath, then he does not have the ability to grip onto the smooth enamel, plastic or porcelain and so he must wait there until rescued by some understanding person, although all too often he gets washed to his doom down the plughole. This is really rather a pity, since the house spider preys upon other much less welcome residents of human habitations, such as flies and earwigs.

It is apparent from discussions with friends and acquaintances that it is the large number of legs and the scuttling habits of spiders in dark corners that scare the majority of folk. After all, apart from the difference in the number of legs, there is little to choose between a furry little kitten and a furry bird-eating spider of similar dimensions; they are both soft to the touch and both can bite, although neither of them seriously. This intense dislike of spiders is even less understandable when one considers that, unlike many of our pets, all but a handful of spiders are completely harmless to human beings. How many readers and their relations and friends have, for example, been savaged by or caught rabies from a spider in the way that they could from man's best friend, the dog, and how many people are all too soon prepared to kill without any thought a spider, which destroys harmful, disease-ridden flies and yet forgive their pet cat when it kills some beautiful bird in the garden? One can perhaps understand the attitude of the housewife to the leaving around of cobwebs in the house, which trap dirt and become unsightly, and it may be this very fact that has resulted in our dread of spiders, an abhorrence of their dirtiness in leaving cobwebs all over the place, leading to a hatred and then a fear of them which is then passed down from one generation to the next. The daughter of one of the authors (R.A.P.-M.), as a baby, had absolutely no fear of spiders but soon learned a dread of them when her mother found her about to put one in her mouth and screamed in dismay, telling her how nasty they were.

Despite the generally adverse feelings of many people towards spiders, they have in many parts of the world become a part of folk myth and legend, perhaps more so than any other arthropod. The very name Arachnida, the arthropod class to which the spiders belong, is derived from the story of the Greek maiden, Arachne, who was so skilled as a weaver that she challenged the goddess Athena to a weaving contest. Athena accepted the challenge and wove a tapestry depicting the majesty of the gods while Arachne wove one depicting the gods' amorous adventures. Arachne's weaving was so good that Athena admitted defeat; however, in a rage, she destroyed Arachne's work, which so upset the maiden that she hanged herself. The goddess then took pity upon her and loosened the rope from around Arachne's neck and the rope then turned into a cobweb and the maiden was turned into a spider, doomed to spend the rest of her life weaving.

On balance, stories told concerning spiders tend to put them in a reasonably favourable light. The Navajo Indians from the USA are well known for the ability to weave fine, colourful blankets and legend has it that they learned this art from a young girl who was taught by the so-called Spider Woman. One stipulation made by this mythical woman was that, to avoid bad luck, all blankets must be woven with a hole in them and, even today, this hole is still left in Navajo blankets. The Spider Woman does, however, possess another side to her character, since the same Indians frighten their children into being good by threatening them that they will be punished by her.

Stories concerning the associations between spiders and good luck and between killing them and bad luck are fairly common, although their origins are usually obscure. That the Scots are deterred from killing spiders is said to have arisen from the often-quoted story of Robert the Bruce, whose observation of the dogged persistence of a spider in constructing a web across the entrance to the cave in which he was hiding is said to have given him the determination to rally his men and go out and defeat the English. Then there is the little rhyme of English origin, but of uncertain age and derivation which says:

> If you wish to live and thrive,
> Let a spider run alive.

The name of money spiders, given in the British Isles to the small, black members of the family Linyphiidae, also relates to good luck. Certainly, as children, the authors were always pleased to find one of these diminutive creatures on their clothes, since they believed that it would bring them good luck in the form of monetary gain.

Perhaps the most famous association between spiders and a human being is that of Miss Muffet and the large spider which frightened her from her tuffet in the well known children's nursery rhyme. The young lady concerned actually existed and was probably the daughter of one Thomas Muffet, a keen spider enthusiast who no doubt instilled either an intense dislike, or perhaps even a tolerance, of spiders in his offspring. Whatever the case may have been, it is apparent that she was dosed with spiders by her father as remedies for the various ills that afflicted her as a child.

In his excellent book on British spiders, Bristowe (1958) quotes further examples of spiders being used medicinally; the house spider, for instance, was considered to be a cure for malaria in the days when the disease was still prevalent in England. He also quotes an afternoon that he himself spent with a lady during which they both sampled various species of spider to see which of them tasted the best. For those readers who may wish to indulge in this gastronomic delight, he records that the orb web spider, *Araneus quadratus* (Plate 1.2), the heaviest British spider, came out on top with its 'slightly nutty flavour'. It cannot be any worse than eating snails or oysters, can it?

Whether they like them, hate them, ignore them or even eat them, to most people, spiders are immediately recognisable by their possession of eight legs, distinguishing them from the insects with their six legs and their wings. The only other creatures with which spiders may be confused are the harvestmen (Fig. 1.2), which are also Arachnids but with the head, thorax and abdomen fused into a single structure rather than the separate cephalothorax and abdomen characteristic of the spiders.

Plate 1.2. *Araneus quadratus*. The smaller male spider in the company of an immature female, with whom he will mate following her final moult to maturity, at which point she will not be in a fit state to harm him. Europe.

Fig. 1.2. A harvestman, an eight-legged relation of the spiders, sitting on an alga-covered tree trunk in an English wood.

Along with the insects, crustaceans and centipedes and millipedes, spiders are members of that group of animals without backbones referred to as the Arthropoda, literally the 'jointed-limbed' animals. Clearly they lack a backbone and instead have an external skeleton, called an *exoskeleton*, which has some similarities to a suit of armour; it is tough and fairly rigid and the muscles are attached to it internally. Like the vertebrate skeleton, that of the arthropods is designed as a compromise between rigidity, to provide support and protection for the soft, delicate internal organs, and flexibility, to allow for ease of movement. The Arthropods are certainly great movers, for they are found in nearly every habitat on earth and have, of course, in the insects, even conquered the air.

Although there are major differences which necessitate classification of the Arthropods into the different classes already mentioned above, the basic organisation of the exoskeleton is similar in all of them. The exoskeleton is, in fact, derived from the animal's skin, or *epidermis*, which consists of a single layer of cells which secrete the *cuticle*, which forms the hard outer covering. The cuticle is very complex in structure since it consists of several layers, one of which contains *chitin*, a lightweight polymer (plastic is a polymer), which gives the skeleton its strength and resilience. The very thick, tough and heavy armour of the crustaceans, such as that of the crabs and lobsters, is a result of the addition of calcium salts to the cuticle, but this extra weight restricts them to an aquatic way of life where the buoyancy of the water provides them with extra support. At some time during its formation, a layer of wax is added to the cuticle to make it waterproof. If the outer layer of the cuticle becomes abraded, it can be repaired by material supplied through pore canals from the epidermis below. It has already been stated that the exoskeleton bears some resemblance to a suit of armour in that rigid plates and tubes alternate with softer, flexible joints. Where joints occur in the exoskeleton, the cuticle is much thinner and is flexible as a result of the addition of a highly elastic protein. The membranes in the region of the joints are only about one-ninth the thickness of the cuticle on the thickest parts of the carapace.

The Arthropods can be considered as perhaps the most successful animals on earth in terms of variety and numbers of individuals. Present estimates are that there may be in excess of 20 million different species of Arthropod in existence, the majority of them being insects, though many of these may never be seen and identified by man as a result of the large-scale habitat destruction which is going on around the world. What is even sadder is that many thousands of species have already been made extinct and man never even knew or cared about their existence. Despite their enormous numbers, the one thing that Arthropods have never achieved is any great size and the reason for this lies in the very nature of the exoskeleton which, because it is fairly rigid and relatively inflexible, has a very limited ability to stretch to accommodate the animal as it grows. Consequently, the exoskeleton has to be shed and replaced at intervals in a moulting process, called *ecdysis*, which tends to place a considerable strain upon the animal's resources. Although a fair proportion of the materials contained in the old exoskeleton are reabsorbed into the animal as the new cuticle is being formed, fresh supplies of raw materials have still to be provided and, for a very large Arthropod, which would have to moult more often than a small one, this would eventually become a biological impossibility. It may seem a pity, or perhaps one should be grateful, but giant ants and spiders will forever be relegated to the realms of the science fiction film.

As well as the spiders and harvestmen, the class Arachnida also includes the scorpions, the ticks (Fig. 1.3) and mites (Plate 1.3), the whip scorpions (Plate 1.4) and the pseudoscorpions (Plate 1.5) and some other less familiar orders. The first fossil Arachnids occur in rocks estimated to be 350 million

Fig. 1.3. A tick with its blood-sucking mouthparts embedded in the eyelid of a South American tapir.

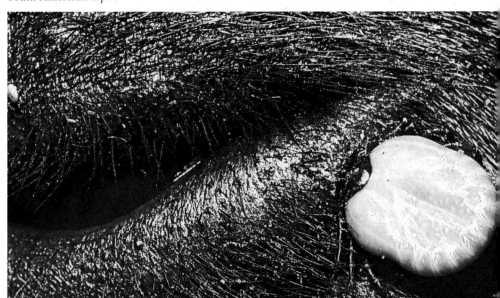

Plate 1.3. An African giant red velvet mite, a relative of the spiders.

Plate 1.4. This whip scorpion from Kenya is, like the spiders, a member of the Arachnida.

Plate 1.5. Although many pseudoscorpions live in the soil, this species lives in association with the harlequin beetle in Trinidad. It hangs onto various parts of the beetle's body and is carried around with it.

years old, where they are represented by some early scorpions, but the earliest spiders are recorded from rocks only 300 million years old. By 250 million years ago, many of today's Arachnid orders had already evolved, although the insects were still in a relatively early stage of their evolution and included only a few flying forms. Most people associate spiders with flies, but in fact the latter did not appear until something like 150 million years ago, so the spiders had to wait for that length of time for them to turn up in their webs.

The fossil record of the spiders is very incomplete, for the simple reason that their rather soft bodies do not fossilise very easily. As a result, the relationships between the Arachnid orders are not at all clear and there is a good deal of argument amongst the experts as to what should and what should not be included within the class. What is certain is that all of the early forms were aquatic and that the earliest Arachnids bore a superficial resemblance to the present-day king crabs, which are doubtfully included in the Arachnida by some authorities. Although it is beyond the scope of this book to go deeply into the realms of Arachnid evolution and taxonomy, the simplest idea so far put forward is that the hypothetical ancestor of the class gave rise to two separate lines, one of which gave rise to the scorpions and the other independently to the other Arachnids, which, if true, means that the scorpions are only very distantly related to the other orders and perhaps should not be included in the Arachnida at all. Those readers who wish to pursue these ideas in depth should refer to Bristowe's detailed accounts of Arachnid evolution.

It will already be clear to some readers from what has gone before that a knowledge of the method of naming spiders is useful in order to fully appreciate the text and, since a following chapter will look at the classification of spiders, it is pertinent to mention the subject here.

Though many of the spider families have a common name, e.g. the Thomisidae are called crab spiders and the Salticidae are known as jumping spiders, relatively few individual species actually have a common name. Those which do are usually unique in some way so that one cannot easily mix them up with another species; the water spider is a good example, since it is the only spider in the world which spends its whole life under water. As a consequence of this lack of common names, individual types of spider described in the text are referred to by their scientific or species name.

The structured form of biological classification which is used worldwide is that developed by the Swede, Linnaeus, during the eighteenth century. In this system, the living world is divided up into a series of sections, each containing organisms with some relationship to each other, the final division being the species. A species is a population of individuals which are very similar to each other and can breed successfully among themselves to produce fertile offspring. Human beings are, of course, a species and, as such, have been given the species name, *Homo sapiens*. Taking then the example of the water spider, it fits into the classification of the animal kingdom in the following way:

KINGDOM	Animalia
PHYLUM	Arthropoda
CLASS	Arachnida
ORDER	Araneae (the spiders)
FAMILY	Agelenidae
GENUS	*Argyroneta*
SPECIFIC NAME	*aquatica*

Thus the species name of this spider is *Argyroneta aquatica*, all such names being in italics in the text. Some genera (plural of genus), unlike *Argyroneta*, contain many species which share a generic name but have their own individual specific names, e.g. the crab spiders, *Xysticus cristatus*, *Xysticus lanio* and *Xysticus kochi*, are closely related spiders in the same genus but *Misumena vatia*, although also a crab spider like the others, is rather different from *Xysticus* and consequently is placed in a separate genus. Bearing these rules in mind the names given to spiders should now be more easily understood.

Chapter 2

Structure of Spiders

External Features

Although they are arthropods, the spiders do not have the typically segmented body of the other groups or indeed of some of the other Arachnid orders. This is not to say that this segmentation is absent, it is just that, as in man, it has become somewhat obscure. The most obvious signs of human segmentation are in the backbone and paired ribs; in the spiders, it is seen as the paired appendages.

Unlike the familiar insects, in which the body is divided into a clearly defined head, thorax and abdomen, in the spiders the head and thorax are fused to form a structure called the *cephalothorax*, which is connected by a narrow waist, or *pedicel*, to the abdomen. In only one primitive living spider family, the Liphistiidae, is the abdomen segmented. Upper and lower views of a typical spider are shown in Fig. 2.1 and should be referred to during the following descriptions of various aspects of spider structure.

When viewed from above, it can be seen that the cephalothorax is covered by a tough plate or shield, the *carapace*, somewhat similar to that of a lobster, and, on this, the line which marks the original division between head and thorax can usually be seen. The most noticeable features of the upper side of the head are the eyes, normally eight, the primitive number but, in some spiders, six, four or two. In one unusual species, there is just one eye derived from the fusion of a pair of eyes. Although to the casual observer all of the eyes appear similar, apart from differences in size, the front pair of eyes originate from the first head segment and the rest from the second segment. There are structural differences between these eyes of different origin and these will be described later (p. 35). The proportions of the cephalothorax generally relate to those of the spider as a whole so that it is long and narrow in long, slim species and broader in broader species. It may also be variously adorned with spikes and lumps and may have grotesque extensions or adaptations in some families, notably in the Linyphiidae, the money spiders (Fig. 2.2).

Viewed from beneath, and working backwards from the front of the spider, the cephalothorax bears the following structures. At the front of the head are the jaws, or *chelicerae* (Fig. 2.3), which are used to deliver the spider's deadly bite. These consist of a stout basal segment, which often bears sharp teeth along the inner edge, and a sharp fang, which hinges onto the

a)

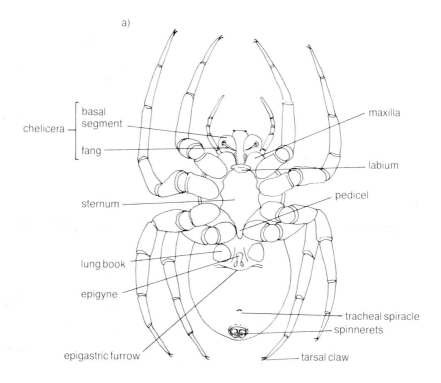

chelicera ⎰ basal segment

fang

maxilla

labium

sternum

pedicel

lung book

epigyne

tracheal spiracle

spinnerets

epigastric furrow

tarsal claw

b)

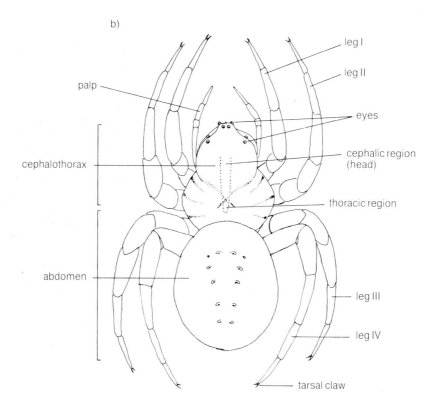

leg I

leg II

palp

eyes

cephalothorax

cephalic region (head)

thoracic region

abdomen

leg III

leg IV

tarsal claw

Fig. 2.1. A generalised spider: a) ventral view b) dorsal view.

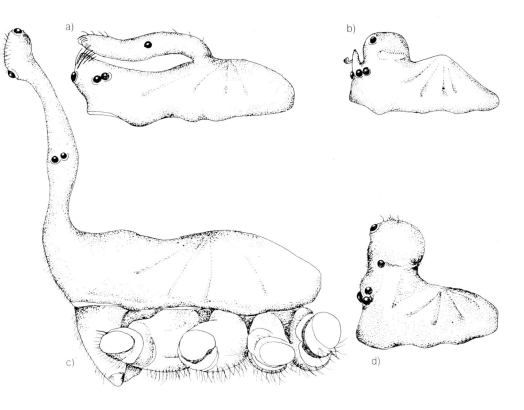

Fig. 2.2. The heads of male money spiders (family Linyphiidae) may assume grotesque shapes, which in some cases are known to aid in mating: a) *Walckenaera furcillata* b) *W. antica* c) *W. acuminata* d) *Peponocranium ludicrum.*

basal segment and is used to pierce the exoskeleton of the prey. These fangs often fit into grooves on the basal segment. The way in which the jaws work is used as a means of separating the more primitive mygalomorph spiders from the more advanced true spiders. In the mygalomorphs, the jaws strike forwards and downwards whereas in the true spiders they are turned through 90° and work from side to side. The difference between these two arrangements may be appreciated by examining Fig. 2.4.

The mygalomorph arrangement is fine for spiders which live mainly at ground level, where the downward thrust of the fangs is opposed by the ground on which the prey is standing. This system is of little use, however, on a leaf or in a web and it is in this situation that the greater span between the fangs, which is possible in the true spiders, comes into its own. Near the end of each fang is a tiny hole, which is connected to the poison sacs, through which the poison is injected into the victim when the spider bites. The poison glands themselves may be contained entirely within the basal segment of the chelicerae or they may extend back into the head; in one family, the Uloboridae, they are absent. Behind the chelicerae is the mouth, on either

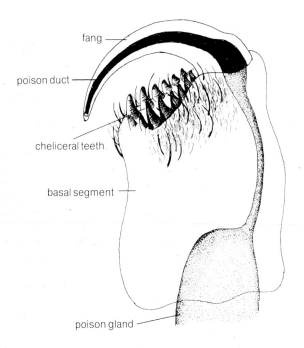

Fig. 2.3. Generalised chelicera of a spider which consists of a basal segment onto which hinge the sharp fang.

Fig. 2.4. Jaw action in: a) a true spider, where the chelicerae pivot from side to side and b) a mygalomorph spider in which the cephalothorax is first raised, with the fangs extended, and the prey is then impaled with a downward motion of the head.

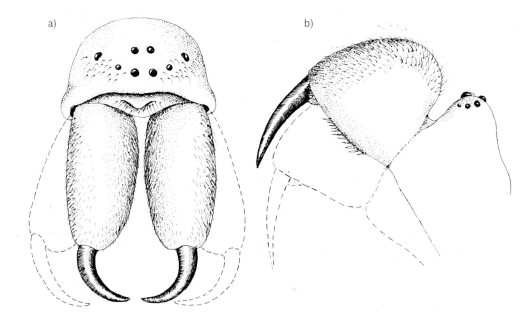

side of which are a pair of accessory jaws, the *maxillae*, derived from the expanded coxal segments of the palps. The maxillae often have serrated edges, used in the manipulation and breaking up of the prey during feeding, and their inner sides have a dense covering of hairs which filter solid particles out of the spider's liquid food. One other important use of the maxillae is in cleaning the spider's legs. The back of the mouth is formed by the *labium* and behind this is the *sternum*, which acts as a base plate for the cephalothorax.

Apart from the chelicerae, the cephalothorax bears five further pairs of appendages: a pair of *pedipalps* (usually abbreviated to palps) and four pairs of legs. The palps are carried on either side of the mouth and bear some resemblance to the legs except that they are smaller and lack a metatarsal segment. In the female spider, they are simple in structure but, in the males, the terminal segment is specially modified for use in mating and can be very complex. Males of each species of spider have distinctive palps which can be used as an aid to identification. The legs of spiders are very similar to those of insects, each being attached to the cephalothorax by the short *coxa*, followed by another short segment, the *trochanter*. Then comes the *femur*, which is equivalent to the human thigh, the *patella*, equivalent to the knee and absent in insects, the *tibia*, equivalent to the human shin and finally the *metatarsus* and *tarsus*, equivalent to the human foot. All of these segments are clearly defined in Fig. 2.5, which shows a typical spider leg.

The tarsal segment may bear either two or three claws, which the spider uses to grip the surface on which it is moving or resting. Three claws are typically found in web-building spiders, the middle one being used in conjunction with the toothed hairs, which oppose it, to hang onto the silken threads of the web (Fig. 2.6). Some spiders have dense tufts of hairs, called *scopulae*, between the claws. The end of each hair is itself subdivided into many tiny hairs so that it resembles a brush; each of these tiny hairs is an extension of the cuticle and is referred to as an *end foot*. There may be as many as a thousand end feet on each scopula hair and it is the capillary action between the flat ends of thousands of end feet and the film of water which coats the surfaces on which the spider moves, that enables these scopula-bearing spiders to walk upon smooth surfaces such as glass. The legs are powered by sets of muscles running within the tubular exoskeleton and these

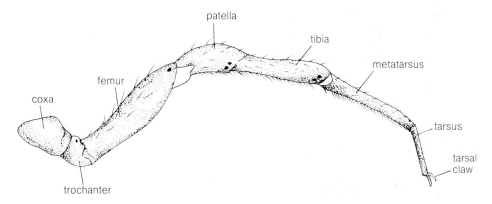

Fig. 2.5. The spider's leg has much the same arrangement as that of an insect but with the addition of the patella.

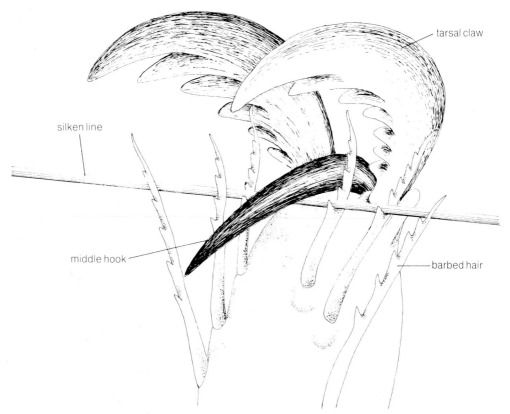

tarsal claw

silken line

middle hook

barbed hair

Fig. 2.6. Thread-grasping. Web-building spiders have a centrally placed third claw which forces the silken line against the serrations on the hairs, allowing the spider to grip tightly onto the smooth silk.

flex and extend the leg sections in much the same way as in human beings, although some of the joints are different and, in spiders, are extended by blood pressure rather than by muscles. Movement about the upper leg joints is in two planes but the lower leg segments can only move in one plane.

The legs may also carry various other structures used in the spider's everyday existence. In the cribellate spiders, for example, the metatarsus on the last pair of legs has a row of hooks, called the *calamistrum*, which is used for combing out the special silk produced by the cribellum of these spiders (p. 39). Similarly the fourth pair of legs in the Theridiidae have, on their tarsi, a row of curved, serrated bristles used to draw sticky silk from the spinnerets and throw it over the prey. Also on the legs are the trichobothria, the slit organs and the tarsal organs, whose functions will be discussed shortly (p. 37).

As already mentioned, the abdomen shows no clear segmentation and it is connected to the cephalothorax via the pedicel through which run the various body systems. The exoskeleton of the abdomen tends to be somewhat thinner than that of the cephalothorax, making it softer and more vulnerable

Plate 2.1. *Gasteracantha arcuata*. A female orb web spider from Malaysia showing the unusual abdominal outgrowths of unknown function typical of this genus.

to damage but allowing it to expand when, for example in the female, it becomes swollen with eggs. Some species may have thick armoured plates on the upper surface while, in others, the abdomen may sport sharp spines or other processes, whose functions are obscure but which impart a weird appearance to the spider (Plates 2.1 & 2.2).

The whole upper surface of the spider may be variously marked, sometimes with very bright but more often with drab camouflage colours, although some of the markings which are visible are a result of the internal organs, e.g. muscle attachments, showing through the thin cuticle.

When viewed from below, several important abdominal structures are visible. Towards the front end is a line running across the abdomen, the *epigastric furrow*, from which, in the mid-line, open the reproductive organs. In front of the reproductive opening in the female is a special structure, the epigyne, which is there to receive the male palps during mating (p. 33). In the same way that males of each species have a unique palp arrangement so the females of each individual species have a unique epigyne, which again can be used as an aid to species identification. The openings into the book

Plate 2.2. *Micrathena* sp. The protrusions on the abdomen of this spider give it a very odd appearance. Central America.

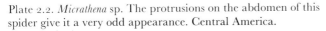

lungs or into the tracheal systems (p. 31), which the spiders use for breathing, are also situated on the underside of the abdomen, their position and numbers varying slightly from family to family. The most prominent features of the abdomen are the *spinnerets*, which mark the external openings of the silk glands and, again, vary in size, number and distribution according to family, a further aid to the identification of a particular spider. Immediately in front of the spinnerets in certain spiders is a special plate, the *cribellum*, containing a row of openings through which many strands of very fine silk are produced. This is used in conjunction with the calamistrum on the hind legs to produce combed-out strands of silk resembling fluffy wool to form the so-called *hackled bands* of their webs.

As well as the distinct structures just discussed, the spider's body may also be covered with an assortment of hairs and spines, which may themselves be coloured and can add to the body patterns mentioned above. The bright colours of the jumping spiders illustrated in this book are mostly due to coloured hairs.

Internal Structure

In common with the majority of animals, spiders have an alimentary canal, a blood vascular system, a breathing system, a means of excreting waste products, a reproductive system and a nervous system with associated sense organs (Fig. 2.7). They also possess a complex set of glands concerned with that most important of spider abilities, the production of silk. It is not the

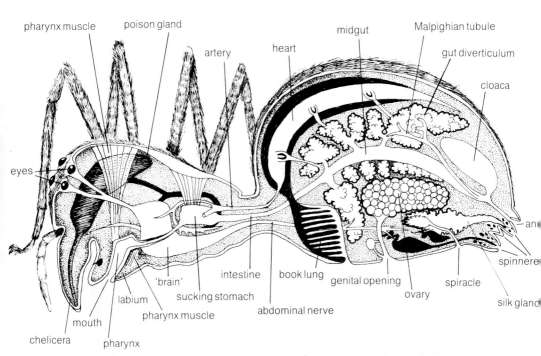

Fig. 2.7. Simplified longitudinal section of a female spider showing the internal anatomy.

intention of this book to discuss these systems in any great detail but, instead, each will be considered under the function that it performs for the spider.

Feeding

It has already been stated that all spiders are carnivores and, with the exception of those that feed on prey caught by other spiders, they all catch and kill their own prey in one way or another. The fangs are used to penetrate the exoskeleton of arthropods and poison is injected to immobilise and kill them. Digestion of the food is initially external, some spiders injecting digestive enzymes into the prey, others crunching up the prey first to expose the soft internal organs and then pouring digestive fluid onto it. Examination of the prey remains of different spiders gives some indication of the feeding method employed; those which inject enzymes into the prey discard its complete empty husk, but those which chew their prey discard a shapeless mass of exoskeleton. The liquid contents of the insect are pumped into the alimentary canal by the spider's *sucking stomach*, any particles in the food being filtered out by the many hairs around the mouth and in the pharnyx. This filtration system is so efficient that it can separate Indian ink particles from the liquid in which they are surrounded. The filtered particles from the ingested food are then washed back out by a stream of digestive fluid. The sucking stomach is an enlargement of the posterior end of the *oesophagus* and attached to it are sets of powerful muscles which perform the sucking action (Fig. 2.8). It is a very efficient pump, capable of sucking up

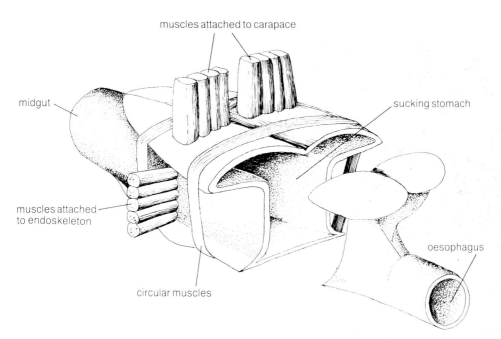

Fig. 2.8. Diagram of the sucking stomach. The sucking action is provided by the contraction of the powerful muscles attached to the wall of the thorax. Once full, the stomach is emptied by action of the circular muscles which force the contents into the midgut.

large quantities of liquid very rapidly, and it is controlled by valves at the entrance and exit to ensure that the liquid food passes backwards down the gut. It is believed that some degree of tasting takes place in the oesophagus, since spiders quickly regurgitate any distasteful food which has been sucked into it.

Following the oesophagus is the *midgut*, the only part of the alimentary canal not lined with cuticle and therefore the only region in which absorption of the digested food can take place. The midgut contains *secretory cells*, which release enzymes to break down further the food arriving from the oesophagus, and *resorptive cells*, which take up tiny globules of liquid food, called *vacuoles*, and continue digestion in their interior. Various sacs, or *diverticula*, branch off the midgut to increase the digestive and absorptive surface area and these may be so extensive that in, for example, the jumping spiders, they penetrate into the cephalothorax and even between the eyes. The midgut finally enters the short *hindgut*, which ends in the *cloacal chamber*, where the faeces are stored until they are voided to the outside through the anal sphincter.

Blood Circulation

The spider's blood system is based upon the typical arthropod pattern and is known as an *open system* because there are no blood capillaries, as in man; instead the blood just pours out of the ends of the arteries directly onto the tissues. The heart consists of a tube running dorsally along the abdomen into which open orifices called *ostia*. Surrounding the heart is a cavity, similar to that surrounding the human heart and also called the *pericardium*. Blood is pumped from the heart into the main arteries which then deliver it to the various organs where it runs freely amongst the tissues. Blood is also pumped to the far ends of the appendages. Having percolated amongst the tissues, the blood then collects in spaces on the ventral surface of the spider's body from where it passes back to the pericardium and through the ostia into the heart. A proportion, but not all, of the returning blood passes through the book lungs if these are present. Flow in one direction only is maintained by the presence of valves at various points in the heart. Because it is an open system, it works at very low pressure and the large spaces mean that, if the body wall is penetrated, the blood leaks out very rapidly and death soon follows.

The blood itself is pale blue in colour due to the presence in it of the oxygen-carrying pigment, *haemocyanin*, although there is at present some disagreement over the actual role of this pigment in spiders, some researchers considering it to be used for oxygen storage rather than for transporting oxygen to the tissues. The blood contains some cells, thought to be mainly concerned with clotting, wound-healing and defence against infection, there being no cells equivalent to the human red cells which transport oxygen. The blood cells themselves are unusual in that they are manufactured by the wall of the heart.

Breathing and Gas Exchange

The breathing mechanism of spiders is somewhat complex in that two separate systems are involved, *book lungs* and *tracheae*. Since book lungs only are found in the more primitive spider families it is assumed that these were the first respiratory mechanisms to evolve and that, in certain more advanced families, some or all of the book lungs were replaced by tracheae. The book lung consists of a chamber in which there is a stack of plates called *lamellae*, separated from each other by pillar-like spigots (Fig. 2.9). Air makes

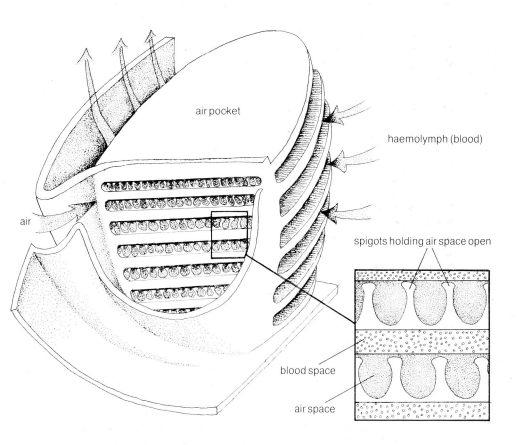

Fig. 2.9. Structure of the book lung. Oxygen from the air in the air spaces diffuses across into the blood, which is on its way back to the heart. The inset shows the way in which the chitinous spigots hold the lamellae bordering the air space open.

its way into the book-lung chamber and between the lamellae; these are hollow and blood flows through them. Gas exchange then takes place between the air and the blood as it flows through the lamellae. Breathing movements equivalent to those in insects have not been observed in spiders and it is therefore likely that gases pass in and out of the book lung by diffusion alone.

The replacement of some or all of the book lungs by tracheae, so-named because of their superficial resemblance to the human trachea or windpipe, is characteristic of the more active spiders with a high metabolic rate. On this basis it would seem that the tracheae must be more efficient at supplying oxygen to the tissues than are the book lungs. The tracheae are tubes, supported by rings of chitin to stop them from collapsing, which run from an opening to the outside, the *spiracle*, directly to the tissues. Unlike the tracheae of insects, they do not branch but, instead, a variable number of tubes may run in parallel to various organs; the number of tubes and their penetration into the cephalothorax vary from family to family.

Excretion of Waste Products

The main excretory organs of spiders are the *Malpighian tubules*, which are somewhat similar to those of the insects in structure and function and they can be thought of as being equivalent to the human kidney. The tubules secrete a slightly acid solution, containing nitrogenous waste products called *guanates* (rather than the urea produced by man), which are moved along to the cloaca by a combination of ciliary action and muscular contraction; from there the waste passes out of the spider's body.

Reproduction

The part of the reproductive system concerned with the production of eggs and sperms is relatively simple in the spiders. The male has a number of testes lying on the floor of the abdomen from which tubes lead to the genital opening in the centre of the epigastric furrow. The female possesses two ovaries from which the oviduct passes to a single uterus and vagina, which opens through the genital pore to the exterior. The female has at least one pair of *spermathecae*, sacs in which sperms from the male are stored until they are required for fertilisation of the eggs at a later date.

Earlier in the chapter, the role of the male's palp in mating was mentioned and this can now be considered in more detail. The actual structure used to pick up the sperm and introduce it into the female is part of the palpal tarsus known as the *cymbium* and this lies in a cavity, the *alveolus*, when not in use. The cymbium in its simplest form consists of an inflatable bulb containing a blind-ended coiled tube, the *spermophore*, which opens to the outside through a stiff spur called the *embolus*. A simple palp showing all of these structures and their relationships to each other is shown in Fig. 2.10. It is the embolus

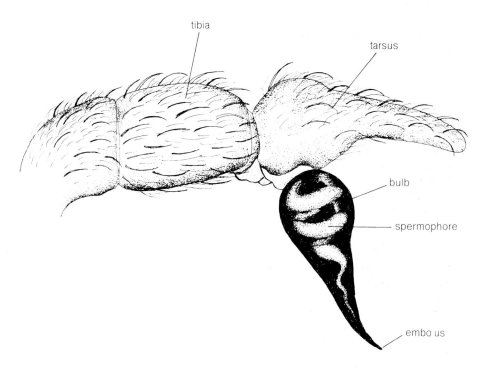

Fig. 2.10. A simple male palp in its inflated state.

which is introduced into the female's copulatory duct which leads to the spermathecae. This copulatory duct is part of the *epigyne*, present in many but not all spiders. This structure is complementary in arrangement to the palp of the male of the same species and is designed to engage with and grip certain parts of the palp to aid the mating process. The male palps and the female epigynes can be extremely complex, so complex that they will not be described here, although a complex palp and epigyne is illustrated in Fig. 2.11. Some idea of the way in which the palp is employed may be gained by close examination of Plate 2.3, where the inflated bulb can clearly be seen. This bulb appears to act like an eye-dropper, first sucking up a drop of sperm which the male has deposited on a special sperm web and then squeezing it in to the female. Exactly how it does this is not yet certain, since blood pressure does not appear to be involved. One theory is that it is pushed out of the embolus by secretions produced at the blind end of the spermophore. Blood pressure is, however, used to inflate the bulb and bring it into use.

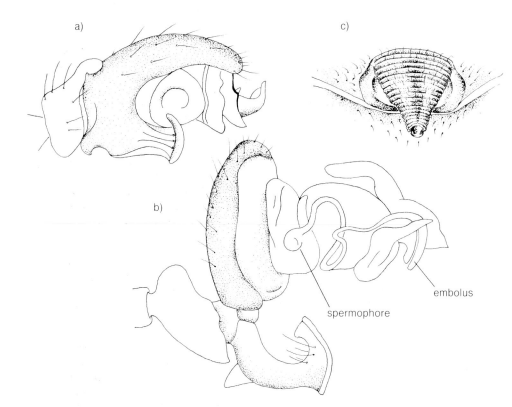

a)

c)

b)

embolus

spermophore

Fig. 2.11. a) The palp of a male Linyphiid in its resting state and b) inflated prior to mating. Although much more complex in appearance than the simple palp it nevertheless has the same basic structure. c) Epigyne of a female *Araneus*.

Plate 2.3. *Araneus quadratus*. This close-up view of the front end of a male shows just how complicated in structure the palps can be. Europe.

Communication with the Environment

This function is carried out by the nervous system and its associated sense organs. The central nervous system of the spiders is very condensed compared with that of other arthropods, with a concentration of nerve cell masses, called *ganglia*, in the cephalothorax, equivalent to the brain and nerve cord, from which nerves pass to all parts of the body, including the sense organs.

The most obvious external sense organs are the eyes, which in most spiders are fairly well developed and, unlike the familiar compound eyes of the insects, those of spiders are simple and are called *ocelli* (Plate 2.4 & Fig. 2.12). There are two types of eye in the spiders:

> 1 *Main eyes* are always the middle pair of the front row of eyes and consist of a *lens*, derived from the cuticle, behind which is a *retina*, made up of cells whose light-sensitive surfaces point towards the incoming light; it is therefore referred to as a *direct retina*. In all spiders, except the jumping and crab spiders, the main eyes are small and they are absent in the six-eyed spiders.
> 2 *Secondary eyes* again have a cuticular lens but, unlike the main eyes, have an *indirect retina* in which the light-sensitive ends of the cells point away from the light, as they do in the human eye. They may also possess a structure called a *tapetum*, which is present in the eyes of some nocturnal mammals to improve their vision at low light intensities, a function it may well perform in the spiders.

The majority of spiders are short-sighted and it is in the jumping spiders

Plate 2.4. *Araneus diadematus*. This frontal view of the spider shows the small eyes, which are of little use apart from being able to detect shadows and the difference between light and dark. Europe.

Fig. 2.12. *Peucetia* sp. Face view of a lynx spider showing the large front eyes which, like those of the jumping spiders, are used to help in finding and pouncing upon prey. Mexico.

that one finds spider vision at its most acute. The main eyes of these spiders are very well developed and they can be seen very clearly in the colour plates of the jumping spiders included in this book. They have a large lens and multiple layers of light-sensitive cells which are backed by a black, light-absorbing pigment layer, as in human eyes. The field of vision is very small but resolution is high, so that they perform like telephoto lenses, giving good vision at a reasonable distance (for them a few centimetres). The retina can be moved to alter the field of vision, whereas human beings, of course, swivel the eyeballs to achieve the same result. At the centre of the retina is the *fovea*, where focussing and vision are at their most acute.

The secondary eyes of the jumping spiders have a much greater field of vision than the main eyes and the outer eyes of the front row endow them with binocular vision, giving them the ability to judge distance, which is most important to them when capturing prey. During hunting, it is the secondary eyes which initially pick up the movement of the prey at a distance and, as it moves closer, the spider turns to face the prey, using the main eyes to focus on it so that it can stalk and finally pounce on it. This accounts for the way in which the common zebra spider, *Salticus scenicus* (Plate 1.1), always turns towards human beings when it detects them and will follow the movements of a finger placed close to it. Research workers have shown the importance of the main eyes to these spiders for, when they are covered with a layer of wax, they miss when jumping.

The receptors concerned with the spider's other senses are much less obvious than the eyes, but are present all the same, although, unfortunately, it requires the use of a microscope to see most of them. As well as being able to taste with the oesophagus, spiders have a 'taste by touch' sense sited on the end segments of the palps and legs. Involved in this sense are specially adapted hollow hairs into which the volatile chemicals to be tasted can enter. It is clear, therefore, that when a spider is manipulating its food with its legs and touching it with the palps, it is also tasting it at the same time. Closely allied to, and perhaps inseparable from, the sense of taste is the sense of smell, which again relies upon the presence of volatile chemicals and, in the spiders, this sense appears to be sited in small openings in the legs called *tarsal organs*.

Spiders certainly gain most information from the outside world by means of their very well developed tactile senses, i.e. their ability to detect vibrations and to feel the nature of an object by touching it. Consequently the outer surface of the spider has a number of different receptors associated with these tactile senses, which probably replace hearing to a great extent since spiders have no ears as such. They are extremely sensitive to vibrations transmitted through the air or through any object or surface upon which they may be standing and, in some ways, this could be interpreted as a form of hearing. Certain spiders do, in fact, produce sounds as a means of attracting members of the oppposite sex and a special stridulatory apparatus for this purpose is found in members of the Theridiid and Linyphiid families of spiders. In the Theridiids, teeth on the abdomen are rubbed on opposing files on the cephalothorax while in the Linyphiids, there is a file on the outer surface of the chelicera against which a tooth situated near to the base of the palp is rubbed. Perhaps the most unusual form of sound communication is that of the male European buzzing spider, *Anyphaena accentuata*, who sits upon a leaf and vibrates his abdomen against it so rapidly that a buzzing sound is produced, audible to the human ear and, of course, to the female, who is readily attracted to it.

The external sense organs concerned with the tactile and other senses are as follows:

1 *Sensory or tactile hairs* are spread all over the body of the spider, each connecting to the nervous system. When they are moved in some way from their resting position, a nerve impulse is triggered and it has been shown by experiment that only one hair needs to be touched to produce a response from the spider. The spines on the legs also have connections to the nervous system but, unlike the hairs, do not seem to be concerned with the sense of touch, since they trigger a nerve impulse only when they become erected by blood pressure. It has been concluded, therefore, that these leg spines are some form of blood pressure detectors.

2 *Trichobothria*, much less numerous than the tactile hairs, are found only on certain leg segments. Each consists of a fine, upright hair inserted into a flexible membrane contained in a socket in the exoskeleton. The hair is able to move at any angle and, since it has several nerves running from its base, it has some directional sensitivity.

37

It is capable of responding to the slightest of air movements, even those produced by insect wings in flight, and the trichobothria are thus referred to as 'touch at a distance' receptors. If they are removed from the spider, it loses its touch at a distance sense to a great extent.

3 *Slit organs* are spread around the exoskeleton and they are concerned with the measurement of changes in stress within the cuticle, produced either by movements of the spider itself, by gravity or by vibrations induced by prey.

4 *Proprioreceptors* are found on the appendages and enable the spider to appreciate the position of its leg segments and their direction of movement when it is in motion.

Although not as apparent as these external sense receptors, the spiders must also have temperature receptors, since they have the ability to regulate their body temperature (*thermoregulation*) to a certain extent and they can, in fact, keep their body temperature above or below that of the surrounding air. The way in which the spider does this is to expose its body to the sun if it wishes to raise its temperature; alternatively it aligns itself to receive the minimum of direct sun if it wishes to keep its temperature down. The spider in Plate 2.5 is doing just this, pointing its abdomen towards the sun so that it exposes the minimum surface area to its heat. In hot climates, orb web spiders often align their webs to reduce their exposure to the sun, whereas orb web spiders in countries where winter temperatures may, just occasionally, fall fairly low, will align their webs so that they are fully exposed to the sun during the day.

In colder climates, where activity during the winter months is absolutely

Plate 2.5. *Hygropoda spuripes*. The stance of this Australian spider, with its abdomen pointed towards the sun, reduces the body surface area exposed to the sun's rays and helps to prevent it overheating.

minimal, the majority of species keep warm by living in the leaf litter of forests and hedgerows or in dense tufts of grasses, sedges and rushes.

Silk Production

Although the production of silk is not unique to the spiders, it is for them an important ability which plays a major part in their everyday life. Silk production probably originally evolved as a means of protecting the eggs from desiccation and predators and only later did it evolve as a major means of capturing prey. The use of silk in the production of the egg-sac and in web-building is described later (Chapters 5 & 6) and what follows is more concerned with the production and nature of the silk itself.

Spiders manufacture not one but several different kinds of silk from the silk or spinning glands in the abdomen. At least seven distinct types of gland have been identified in the range of spider families, although no single family has been found to have all seven types. The glands are named on the basis of their structure and each produces a different kind of silk for a specific purpose, e.g. the *aciniform glands* are found in all spiders and manufacture the silk used for wrapping the prey, while the *cylindrical glands* are used to make the egg-sac and are sometimes missing in the males of a species. The *cribellar glands* are found only in the cribellate spiders, whose cribellum and calamistrum have already been described. These glands, which manufacture the hackled band of the cribellate web, secrete an exceedingly fine, slightly sticky thread, which is combed out with the calamistrum and then combined with normal silk to form a very fluffy-looking band in which the legs of the prey become entrapped.

Silk is a protein which is produced by the silk glands in the form of a liquid, which is squeezed out of the spinnerets like toothpaste out of a tube. The spinnerets can be likened to hollow fingers, from the ends of which the silk oozes and, since they are very mobile, they can pull and manipulate the silk as it emerges. The liquid silk hardens as it leaves the spinneret and it is believed that this hardening is brought about by the spider pulling on the silk as it is produced, the more it is pulled, the stronger it becomes. Silk is an amazing substance in that some types are stronger than a steel thread of the same diameter, while some are capable of stretching to nearly twice their original length before they break.

To the naked eye, most silk appears to be a single thread, but this is actually not the case since the strands that are visible may consist of larger numbers of finer, individual threads lying alongside one another. The finest single strands of silk are about 0.00003 mm (about $\frac{1}{1\,000\,000}$ in) in diameter, and even the larger strands have a diameter only about four times greater.

Chapter 3

Classification of Spiders

At present, somewhere in excess of 30 000 species of spiders have been described, belonging to about seventy different families, although the latter figure differs somewhat between one authority and another. As mentioned in the Preface, it is not the aim of this chapter to describe all of these families in detail but rather to describe a representative sample of those whose members are more likely to be seen by the well travelled amateur naturalist. There are, for example, some families whose members are very small and live under stones while others live exclusively in caves and, therefore, are likely to be found only by spider experts who know precisely where to look.

The smallest spider family is the Amaurobioididae, with one species from the southern hemisphere, which is very unusual in that it lives in a silken nest in the intertidal zone of the sea shore, a habitat normally inaccessible to the majority of terrestrial organisms. In comparison, the largest family is that of the jumping spiders, the Salticidae, which contains over 4000 species and has representatives in most parts of the world.

For convenience, the spiders are divided into three sub-orders on the basis of their structure and relationships and it is within these sub-orders that the various families are found.

Sub-order Mesothelae

The Mesothelae are a very ancient group of spiders, thought by the experts to be the group from which the other two existing sub-orders evolved. The only surviving family within the sub-order is the Liphistiidae, which contains about nine species from South-East Asia and Japan. Their most obvious feature is that they alone amongst present-day spiders have a segmented abdomen. They live in a burrow, covered by a trapdoor, from the entrance of which radiate threads, which act as trip wires to inform the occupant of the arrival of prey. Being underground-dwellers, they are not often seen unless specifically dug out for the purpose, although the entrance to their burrow is quite conspicuous.

Sub-order Orthognatha

This is the sub-order whose members are collectively referred to as the

Fig. 3.1. A ground-dwelling mygalomorph spider from Peru.

mygalomorph spiders (Fig. 3.1). They are probably familiar to many people as the so-called tarantulas of the USA (the true tarantulas are members of the Labidognatha, family Lycosidae), the bird-eating spiders, the dreaded funnel web spiders of Australia and, to picture-goers, as the great hairy monster that the hero finds crawling across his face or arm ready to deliver the deadly bite. Although the larger species are quite fearsome to look at, and they can inflict a painful bite if handled carelessly, only the funnel web species can be considered as really dangerous to man. Some of them are quite small and insignificant while others, e.g. the Mexican red-kneed spider, have become common as pets, adversely affecting the natural populations.

The mygalomorphs are a relatively primitive group and comprise eleven families. They can be recognised by the way in which the chelicerae are joined to the front of the head and consequently strike forwards and down in use (Fig. 2.4a and Plate 3.1). The majority of mygalomorphs are burrowers; those with a door to the burrow entrance are referred to as trapdoor spiders and those with a silken funnel at the entrance as funnel web spiders, although these are not the same as the funnel-web-building members of the Labidognath family, the Agelenidae. The purse web mygalomorphs live in a sealed silken tube, the lower end of which runs down into the burrow, while the upper end lies along the ground or is stuck to the trunk of a tree and extends for several centimetres. Some of the group are free-living and these include some of the world's biggest spiders, belonging to the family Theraphosidae. These giants of the spider world may attain a body length of 90 mm ($3\frac{1}{2}$ in) with a spread across the legs of 280 mm (11 in), making them large enough to be able to take and feed on vertebrate prey in some instances. As with the next sub-order, many aspects of the different life styles of the mygalomorph families will be discussed in the following chapters.

Plate 3.1. (Overleaf) A male Australian trapdoor spider in the defensive pose typical of the mygalomorph spiders. The forward and downward striking chelicerae show up clearly.

Sub-order Labidognatha

These are sometimes referred to as the true spiders and they comprise by far the majority of existing spider species. They are separated from the previous two sub-orders on the basis of the chelicerae, which are attached below the head and are used in a sideways action, giving them their greater biting span (Fig. 2.4b). Whereas the mygalomorphs have only book lungs for breathing, tracheae have also evolved in the true spiders.

The Labidognatha can be conveniently subdivided into two sections: the ecribellate spiders and the cribellate spiders. The latter are characterised by the possession of a cribellum and a calamistrum for the production of their specialised hackled band silk.

Ecribellate Spiders

As the heading implies, these spiders lack a cribellum and the group contains by far the largest number of individual spider families. The experts sub-divide them into two groups on the basis of the complexity of the male palp, but this division will not be considered here.

FAMILY OONOPIDAE This is a family of tiny spiders, mostly under 3 mm ($\frac{1}{8}$ in) in length, with six eyes, which inhabit the leaf litter of tropical forests or live under logs and stones. They are often brightly coloured, orange, yellow or pink, and some are white. The two British species are pink, one of them, *Oonops domesticus*, as its name implies, having become a fellow traveller of man by making use of the new environments provided by his homes and outbuildings, moving with him when he moves. This minute pink spider, the largest individuals just attaining 2 mm (less than $\frac{1}{8}$ in) in length may often be seen on the walls and ceilings of English homes, where it moves around in short, sharp dashes. It is an endearing species, but how such a tiny creature is able to find sufficient food on the vast extents of walls and ceilings defeats the imagination.

FAMILY DYSDERIDAE Like the Oonopidae, with which they are sometimes grouped, the Dysderids have six eyes but, to the casual observer, it is there that the similarities between the two end. Typical of the family is *Dysdera crocata* (Plate 3.2), a species with a wide distribution around the world, both naturally and due to its having been introduced into such countries as the USA and Australia by man. It is a rather sinister-looking spider, reaching a maximum length of about 15 mm ($\frac{5}{8}$ in) with brick-red carapace and legs and a pale grey tubular abdomen. It spends its day under stones, especially where these will be warmed by the sun, living in a silken cell in which the female usually lays her eggs. Most noticeable are its enormous fangs, which it uses to impale the woodlice which form its staple diet.

Ariadna from Australia and the USA is also placed in this family on the basis of its body structure but, unlike the typical Dysderids, it builds a tough silken tube in a crevice or hole from which radiate trip threads. This form of prey capture is more typical of the Segestriidae, into which family it is placed by some arachnologists.

FAMILY SCYTODIDAE The Scytodidae are referred to as the spitting spiders, due to the way in which they spit out two streams of sticky glue from their fangs, which immobilise their prey. They possess six eyes and have a domed carapace which accommodates the large glue-producing glands. The majority of the 200 members of the family are tropical or sub-tropical and are relatively little known. The best known species is *Scytodes thoracica* (Fig. 3.2), a pretty spider with a worldwide distribution, living as it does in man's habitations. More will be said later about this species under the heading of prey capture (p. 136).

Plate 3.2 *Dysdera crocata*. This striking spider is the one member of the family Dysderidae most likely to be met with on account of its worldwide distribution.

© C. Twissell

Fig. 3.2. *Scytodes thoracica*. A female spitting spider showing the domed cephalothorax which contains the gum-producing glands. Europe and USA.

FAMILY LOXOSCELIDAE This family of rather drab, brown, six-eyed spiders, which use an untidy web to catch their prey, contains a small number of species from the Americas, Africa and Europe and it has been introduced into Australia. The Loxoscelids have gained notoriety as a result of the unfortunate effects of their biting of human beings.

FAMILY PHOLCIDAE The Pholcids are often called daddy-longlegs spiders, since their relatively small bodies and very long legs give them a superficial resemblance to those long-legged insects, the craneflies. They usually have eight eyes, although this is reduced to six in some species and the eyes may be reduced in size or absent altogether in some cave-dwelling species. The family is a fairly large one, with about 500 species worldwide, mostly in the warmer areas of the world but it is also fairly well represented in temperate regions. As with many other families of spiders, the member of the Pholcidae which one is most likely to see is a species which lives with and has been spread around the world by man. *Pholcus phalangioides* is fairly common in homes and outbuildings in the British Isles, the USA and in Australia, where it builds an untidy web in dark corners, although its distribution within these countries is somewhat temperature dependent, i.e. it is seldom found in situations where the average temperature throughout the year is less than 10°C (50°F). *Pholcus* can hardly be mistaken for any other spider with its slim body, attaining about 10 mm ($\frac{3}{8}$ in) in length, and with the second pair of legs as much as five or six times longer.

FAMILY HERSILIIDAE The fifty or so members of this family are mainly tropical in distribution and are found almost exclusively upon the trunks of trees, where their colouration matches that of the bark. They are easily recognised by their long legs and their very long posterior spinnerets, which may be as long as the abdomen and which give them the common name of two-tailed spiders. When disturbed, the Hersiliids will run in short bursts round to the opposite side of the tree, with their tails raised like a pair of horns, where they again press their flattened body against the bark, showing little in the way of a shadow and thus becoming virtually invisible. They do not build a web but, instead, hunt actively on the surface of the tree, using their spinnerets to leave a life-line behind them.

FAMILY THERIDIIDAE This is one of the larger spider families with over 2500 species so far described. They have a worldwide distribution and number the notorious widow spiders of Europe, the USA and Australia amongst their members. They are relatively small spiders with a globular abdomen and they typically produce rather untidy-looking but highly functional scaffolding webs, although some species hunt on the ground. They have a row of stout bristles on the last pair of legs, used for flinging silk over the prey, giving them the common name of comb-footed spiders. There are many interesting aspects to the lives of the members of this family which will be discussed in due course.

FAMILY LINYPHIIDAE The second largest of the spider families with over 3500 species, the Linyphiidae are commonly referred to as the dwarf spiders, due to their generally very small size, although in the British Isles, of course, they are called money spiders. In the temperate zones of the world, they are by far the commonest spiders, although, because of their small size, they are not often seen, except perhaps on warm summer and autumn days when they may disperse aerially in countless millions. They build sheet webs beneath which the spider hangs and above the sheet are scaffolding strands. Insects blunder into these and then fall onto the sheet, where they are taken and eaten by the spider. Many of the smaller species are black but some of the larger ones may be black, white and brown with traces of other colours. At least one species, *Floronia bucculenta* from Europe, has the ability to undergo an immediate colour change when disturbed, a rare if not unique ability amongst spiders, although slow colour changes occur in the crab spiders.

FAMILY ARANEIDAE (ARGIOPIDAE) Although the name Araneidae is now preferred for this large, worldwide family of over 2500 species, in much of the older literature on spiders they are called the Argiopidae, hence the alternative name in the heading. These are the orb web spiders (Plate 3.3), which are probably as familiar to most people as any spiders, although by no means all of them actually build a web as such. In some, such as the bolas spider, the web has been reduced to a single strand of silk with a sticky globule on the end. They vary greatly in size; some species of *Singa*, for example, scarcely exceed 2 mm (less than $\frac{1}{8}$ in) in length while some of the tropical *Nephila* species exceed 50 mm (2 in) in length and have been

45

recorded as catching and killing small birds in their enormously strong webs. Like the Uloboridae, Araneids such as *Nephila* and *Argiope* string a conspicuous stabilimentum across the centre of their webs. The familiar garden spiders of Europe, the USA and Australia are members of this family.

FAMILY TETRAGNATHIDAE Sometimes included in the Araneidae, the Tetragnathids are also orb-web builders but have sufficient structural peculiarities for them to be in their own family. About fifty species have been described and, in the British Isles, there are nine species belonging to three different genera, two of these species also being found in the USA. The Tetragnathids probably arose from the same ancestral stock as the Araneids but the former have retained the simple form of male palp and the female lacks an epigyne. Typical of the family are members of the genus *Tetragnatha*, often but not invariably associated with damp, swampy habitats. These spiders have long, slim bodies, the common British and American species, *Tetragnatha extensa*, attaining a length of up to 11 mm ($\frac{7}{16}$ in), and long legs and, when not in their webs, they lie characteristically stretched out along a grass stem where their colour, posture and immobility hide them from possible predators. This habit has given them one common name of grass spider but they are sometimes also called big-jawed spiders, a deserving name, since their large jaws are an outstanding feature, especially in the male, whose special use of them during mating will be discussed later (p. 76).

FAMILY MIMETIDAE A worldwide family with about one hundred species, the Mimetidae are commonly called pirate spiders. They are small spiders, seldom exceeding a few millimetres in size, with a typically globular abdomen and they rely upon their slow, stealthy movements to enter the webs of other spiders and to prey upon them.

Plate 3.3. *Argiope argentata*. A very attractive orb web spider from tropical America also found in the south of the USA.

FAMILY AGELENIDAE These are the other funnel web spiders, not to be confused with the mygalomorph funnel-web-builders described earlier. They build a flat sheet web amongst rocks or vegetation from which runs a tubular retreat, the whole resembling a very wide-mouthed funnel. The spider lies in wait in the retreat and rushes out to grab any insect which falls onto the sheet part of the web. The family contains around 1000 species, the most familiar members almost certainly being the house spiders of the genus *Tegenaria*. These are the large, long-legged, hairy spiders which have the bad habit of falling into people's baths, from where they are unable to extricate themselves. One very important exception to the normal Agelenid way of life is that of the water spider, *Argyroneta*, which has become so dependent upon water that it spends all of its life below the surface of lakes and ponds, living in a silken bell (Fig. 6.3), filled with air collected from the surface, and feeding upon water organisms.

FAMILY PISAURIDAE These eight-eyed hunting spiders do not build a web but pursue prey actively on the ground, in vegetation or, in some cases, on the surface of lakes and ponds. These latter species are called fishing spiders because they have actually been seen to dip the end of a leg into the water to act as a lure and then pounce on small fish which have been attracted to it. As a family, they are called nursery web spiders, because the female carries her large egg-sac attached to the spinnerets under her abdomen and held at the front in her jaws (a diagnostic feature of this family) and when the eggs are about to hatch, builds a nursery tent in which to guard the young spiders until they hatch. The family contains about 400 species.

FAMILY LYCOSIDAE Along with the mygalomorph spiders, the Lycosidae hunt mainly on the ground, using the keen sight provided by their large, forward-pointing eyes. They have been given the common name of wolf spiders; unlike their mammalian namesakes, they do not hunt in packs, but they may be found in large numbers in suitable habitats. They are found in fields and gardens, amongst the leaf litter of woodland and forest, on sand dunes and in deserts. Some species live on the muddy surface of salt marshes and others spend their lives running around on the surface of still waters actively hunting. Therefore, any spider found running around on the ground, especially when it is sunny, is likely to be a wolf spider.

The largest members of the family belong to the genus *Lycosa* and include the true tarantulas from Europe. These are supposedly dangerous to man in whom tissue necrosis can occur round the area of a bite, but in practice are rarely so on account of their retiring habits, for these spiders spend much of their life in burrows. The burrow is closed by means of a trapdoor and, behind this, the spider waits for passing prey. Alternatively it may leave the burrow to look for prey in the surrounding area. These large wolf spiders may attain a length of 40 mm ($1\frac{1}{2}$ in), making them amongst the biggest of the true spiders.

47

In the wide range of habitats above, but taking smaller prey than the species of *Lycosa*, are the small, dull-coloured spiders of the genus *Pardosa* (included in the genus *Lycosa* in some older textbooks). They are very common in some habitats in Europe and the USA, but the largest of the British species, for example, does not exceed 10 mm ($\frac{3}{8}$ in) in body length, while the species of *Pirata*, which are somewhat similar in appearance, are smaller still. Perhaps the most interesting species in Britain is *Pirata piscatorius*, which should be looked for amongst sphagnum moss, where it builds a silken tube above the moss which leads down into the water below. At the top of the tube is an opening from which the spider sallies forth to hunt its prey amongst the moss but, if danger threatens, the spider retreats down the tube and below the surface of the water to safety.

Like the nursery web spiders, the female wolf spiders who live above ground carry their egg-sacs around with them, attached to their spinnerets only and leaving their jaws free to catch prey. When the young hatch, the females carry them around on their backs for a while.

FAMILY OXYOPIDAE The Oxyopids, or lynx spiders to give them their common name, are active hunters, mainly upon vegetation, where they use their sharp eyesight to help them to find their prey, as they run rapidly along leaping nimbly from leaf to leaf. They rest at intervals, flattening themselves against a leaf and, since many of them are green in colour, they are well camouflaged against predators in this situation. They have a wide distribution round the world, although the 500 or so species have a preference for warmer climes and there is only one rare species in the British Isles, although the family is fairly well represented in the USA and in Australia.

Fig. 3.3. A female Ctenid wandering spider from Kenya carrying her egg-sac.

FAMILY CTENIDAE Bearing some resemblance to the wolf spiders but apparently not closely related, these large tropical species (Fig. 3.3) are the vagrants of the spider world, a habit which has earned them the name of wandering spiders. They are, like the three preceding families, active hunters, seeking their prey on the ground or amongst low vegetation. Although they have much the same habits as the wolf spiders, and much the same colouration, one distinguishing feature is the tufts of hairs which are found on various parts of the body. Their real claim to fame is that the Ctenid, *Phoneutria fera*, from Brazil possesses one of the most toxic of all spider venoms and is certainly the most dangerous South American spider.

Fig. 3.4. *Herpyllus blackwalli*. The European mouse spider, a member of the Gnaphosidae often to be found in human habitations.

FAMILY GNAPHOSIDAE A widespread family of about 2000 species, the Gnaphosids are nocturnal hunters and, during the day, are most often to be found under stones or logs, although some species now share man's habitations. Once such spider is *Herpyllus blackwalli* (Fig. 3.4), a European species known in Britain as the mouse spider and now well established in the USA, where it has almost certainly been introduced by man. In general, the family consists of rather drab brown or black spiders, although a few species

49

Plate 3.4. *Supunna* sp. Although most Clubionids are very drab, this Australian species shows how strikingly marked some members of this family can be.

do exhibit brighter colours, and, although not particularly large, some species of *Drassodes* may reach 25 mm (1 in) in length.

FAMILY CLUBIONIDAE The Clubionids superficially resemble the previous family and are also similar in their numbers and world distribution. They

Plate 3.5. *Myrmecium* sp. This ant-mimicking Clubionid closely resembles ants which live in the same tropical habitat.

tend, however, to be less flattened than the Gnaphosids and cover a greater variety of habitats in that many of them dwell upon plants. Under the microscope, they can be distinguished by the arrangement of the front pair of spinnerets, which in the Clubionids are conical and touching and in the Gnaphosids are cylindrical and separated. While many of the family are drab brown in colour, with little in the way of markings, there are some

Plate 3.6. A large huntsman or giant crab spider of the family Sparassidae which lives cryptically on the trunks of trees in Malaysian forests.

brightly coloured and strikingly marked species (Plate 3.4) and also some incredibly good ant mimics, so good that they can truly be mistaken for the real thing (Plate 3.5). The family also contains one genus, *Chiracanthium*, whose members should be handled with some caution, since they are venomous to man.

FAMILY SPARASSIDAE (HETEROPODIDAE) Another fairly large family with around 1000 species, the Sparassidae may also be called the Heteropodidae in some literature. They are commonly referred to as the huntsman spiders, although the larger ones are known as giant crab spiders (Plate 3.6) and are mainly tropical in their distribution. They tend to be somewhat flattened in appearance and the legs are often turned outwards in such a way that they all end up pointing forwards, modifications which allow them to slip under

51

loose bark or stones to hide when they are not hunting. They are fairly large spiders, some of the *Isopoda* species from Australia attaining a body length of 30 mm ($1\frac{1}{16}$ in).

The only British species is *Micrommata virescens*, whose bright emerald green female, reaching a length of 12 mm (nearly $\frac{1}{2}$ in), may be found on low vegetation, mainly in the southern half of England. Occasionally the widespread tropical *Heteropoda* species may be found in consignments of bananas and it is probably for this reason, as a fellow traveller of man, that these particular spiders have achieved their present distribution. *Heteropoda* is, in fact, an important controlling agent of insect pests in many tropical households and is accepted in them, despite its rather sinister appearance.

Somewhat similar in appearance to the Sparassids are the family Selenopidae, the Selenopid crab spiders, a small family whose individuals are even more flattened than the Sparassids and live in similar habitats.

FAMILY THOMISIDAE Because of their similarity in shape to crabs and their sideways scuttling movements, the Thomisids are referred to as crab spiders. They are a very large family with around 3000 species and a worldwide distribution and, in certain habitats, some of them may be extremely common. A proportion of these spiders sit on flowers awaiting the arrival of unwary insects and, accordingly, they may be coloured to match the flower, the bright pink *Thomisus onustus* from Europe being a good example. More often, however, they are more drably dressed in browns and blacks and sit on vegetation or on the ground, where they often blend in well with their surroundings. In general, they are small spiders, seldom exceeding 10 mm ($\frac{3}{8}$ in), with small chelicerae, and they rely upon stealth and a potent poison to catch their prey.

One or two members of the family, e.g. *Tibellus*, are somewhat atypical, having long, slim bodies, but apart from this they are typical crab spiders. One section of the family, a group composed of fairly active hunters rather than spiders which wait in ambush for their prey, are placed in a sub-family while in some literature they have been elevated to their own family, the Philodromidae. The long-legged members of the genus *Philodromus* are typical of this section of the family and the males are often so different from the females that they could be mistaken for another species.

FAMILY SALTICIDAE Last, but by no means least, since they are the world's largest spider family with over 4000 species, come the jumping spiders, as the Salticids are commonly called. They are small spiders, the largest gravid females seldom exceeding 15 mm ($\frac{5}{8}$ in) while the majority of species are 5 mm ($\frac{3}{16}$ in) or less. Their most obvious feature, apart from their jumping ability, is their large front eyes which are clearly visible even with the naked eye. It is these large eyes in the centre of their faces which give them their rather endearing look, resembling as they do some of the large-eyed monkeys. The size and arrangement of these eyes enables them to see clearly over a distance of several centimetres, allowing them to spot prey at a distance before stalking and leaping upon it.

The majority of temperate species are rather sombrely clad but the males especially of many tropical spiders are bedecked with iridescent hairs of many colours and are beautifully patterned, which makes them veritable peacocks amongst the other spiders (Plates 3.7 & 8). It is also amongst the Salticids that one finds ant mimics as deceptive as those found in the Clubionidae. Unlike the other members of the family, these mimics do not jump but instead run around in an ant-like fashion on the ground in such a way that they can hardly be distinguished from the ants that accompany them.

Cribellate Spiders

FAMILY ERESIDAE The Eresids are a family whose members live in the Old World, i.e. Europe, Africa and Asia. They are relatively large, hairy spiders (the female of the European *Eresus niger*, for example, may attain a body length of 12 mm or $\frac{1}{2}$ in) and they construct a funnel-shaped web radiating out from a short, silk-lined burrow.

Eresus niger males are very striking with their black cephalothorax marked with scarlet along the edge, their black legs with white rings and their bright scarlet abdomen, which bears three pairs of black spots ringed with white hairs. Although quite likely to be met with in continental Europe, they are very rare in the British Isles, having been recorded from a few localities on coastal heathland in the south-west.

FAMILY DICTYNIDAE The Dictynid spiders are generally very small, seldom exceeding 4 mm ($\frac{1}{8}$ in) in length, although one Australian species does reach 16 mm ($\frac{5}{8}$ in) and some cave spiders from this family may have a leg spread of up to 77 mm (3 in), although they may have small bodies. The 500 or so species of this family have a wide distribution, mainly in the temperate zones of the world, and, despite their small size, they are likely to be found by many people since, in some habitats, for example rough grassland, they can be very common. Typically, they make an untidy web on grass or other vegetation at the centre of which the males and females may be found together in a chamber which, interestingly, is usually constructed by the male. They are normally drab greys and browns in colour although a few may have bright spots of colour.

FAMILY AMAUROBIIDAE Some arachnologists include the Amaurobiids within the previous family, with which they have many features in common. They tend however, to be larger in size and are in the main ground-dwellers, building an irregular funnel web under stones or in the crevices between them. Like the Dictynidae, they are generally rather drab spiders, dressed in

Plates 3.7 & 8. These two jumping spiders show the bright colours typical of these jewels of the world's tropical forests. Trinidad.

shades of grey and brown and about 350 species have been described from around the world.

Members of the genus *Amaurobius* are not uncommon in houses in northern temperate zones, both *Amaurobius similis* and *Amaurobius ferox* being found in this situation in the British Isles. These particular spiders are dark in colour and this and their skull-like abdominal markings gives them a rather sinister appearance.

FAMILY ULOBORIDAE This family contains the mainly tropical and subtropical feather-legged spiders of the genus *Uloborus* and the northern temperate triangle spiders of the genus *Hyptiotes*. They are unique amongst the spiders in that they do not possess venom glands and rely entirely upon their webs and chelicerae to catch and subdue their prey. *Uloborus* builds a horizontal orb web, similar to but not as refined as that of the Araneids, across which is woven a band of silk from the cribellum called the stabilimentum. The British *Uloborus* is a solitary species but members of the genus from the USA and Mexico, and also from Australia, build communal webs in which both sexes and young individuals live together. Another member of the genus has adopted a commensal way of life. The triangle spiders will be discussed in detail again later when their unusual web is considered as a means of prey capture (p. 130).

FAMILY DINOPIDAE These are usually referred to as the stick spiders on account of their shape or ogre-faced spiders on account of the pair of enormous posterior median eyes that they possess. These very large eyes resemble a pair of headlamps and are used in this spider's very individual form of hunting, in which a web is thrown over the prey, like a net, in order to capture it. The family is small with about sixty tropically and sub-tropically distributed species.

* * *

In this chapter, the mygalomorph families have not been listed and only twenty-six of the true spider families have been included. For those readers who are interested, a comprehensive listing of all of the spider families is included at the end of the book.

Chapter 4
Courtship and Mating

The life of the immature spider is devoted entirely to the capture of prey, whether by active pursuit, as in the wolf and jumping spiders, by stealthy ambush, as in the crab spiders, or by the use of a silken snare in the web-building spiders. These immature individuals are, for all practical purposes, sexless and males and females are very difficult or impossible to separate, since the male palps and female epigyne are still non-functional and do not develop their characteristic structure and shape until the final moult into the adult spider. In some spiders, however, immature individuals can be sexed on the basis of size since, in these species, the male never grows beyond a certain size so that any larger spider will be a female, this being particularly true of many orb web spiders. In other cases, as in many birds, the male will be much more vividly patterned and coloured than the rather drab female. Brightly coloured males are particularly characteristic of many jumping spiders, especially in the tropics, where the two sexes have often been described as belonging to different species, so different are they in colour and pattern (Plate 4.1). Sexual dimorphism in colour does occur in other spiders, an example being the large American purse web spider, *Atypus bicolor*, whose male, with his glossy ebony body and red legs, contrasts markedly with the drab brown female.

There is an excellent and logical basis in evolutionary terms for sexual dimorphism based on size. The female's body will have to function as a container for the developing eggs and, when they are laid, she will have to construct a protective silk covering for them and then, perhaps, will have to guard both eggs and newly hatched spiderlings. All of these functions are likely to be carried out more efficiently by a large female, who can carry a greater number of eggs within her body and will protect them more effectively from enemies if she is a large and powerful adversary. Once mated, the female is the originator and protector of the next generation of her species and it is therefore also of advantage for her colours to be drab and thus to act as camouflage, a reason for sexual dimorphism based on colour.

The male, on the other hand, is far more dispensable than his mate, for only one male is capable of mating with a succession of females, so, as individuals, male spiders tend to be something of a luxury, their sole function being to provide sperm for the fertilisation of the eggs. Unlike the hard-working cock of many of our garden birds, the male spider takes no share in feeding his offspring nor does he provide any protection for them or his mate.

He will, in fact, never be able to recognise his own progeny and may even end up eating them. In view of his superfluous nature in any role save that of providing the fertilising sperm for the eggs, he has become something of a specialist for that single role, which often makes the severest demands upon both his skill and courage. In order to achieve his single purpose in life, he has to enter into a veritable lion's den occupied by his fearsome potential mate, who may of course be many times larger than he is. Nevertheless, the urge which sends him in pursuit of the female is so powerful that it occupies virtually the whole life of a mature male, who has, however, evolved a number of methods to ensure his survival should his attentions be resisted by the female. These include fleeing abruptly from her company or even overpowering her on some occasions.

The males of many spiders do not, at first glance, appear to be particularly specialised for their roles but, nevertheless, essential modifications are apparent upon closer examination. Taking the ground-dwelling hunting spiders as an example, it will be seen that, although both sexes are very

Fig. 4.1. *Argiope* sp. This species from New Guinea clearly shows the difference in size between the female and her diminutive mate.

Plate 4.1. This pair of mating jumping spiders, with the male above, illustrates how it was that each sex, because of its totally different colouration, was originally described as a different species. Trinidad.

similar in size and length, the male has a slimmer abdomen and may have some difference in his overall markings. A frequent difference between the sexes is that the males often have longer legs; this occurs both in spiders which run around a lot and also in web-builders. The possession of these longer legs gives the males the advantage of having a greater range of sensory perception and also allows them to keep their aggressive mates at 'arm's length'. It is also possible that having longer legs is an advantage to the males in their wanderings to find a mate, or several mates, so that they spread their genes as widely as possible within the population.

It has already been said that the greatest difference between the sexes is the disparity in size, this being especially noticeable in the orb web spiders. The female of the European garden spider, *Araneus diadematus*, usually attains about 12 mm ($\frac{1}{2}$ in) in length while the male is only about half this size. *Araneus illaudatus* in the USA has females which can reach 30 mm (1 in) in length with the males seldom greater than one-sixth of the female's size. There are numerous species of attractive members of the genus *Argiope* around the world and the tiny male, often less than one-quarter the size of the female, can often be found skulking in the top part of her web (Fig. 4.1).

The greatest disparity in size, however, is found in the giant *Nephila* species, which may be a conspicuous feature of tropical environments. The massive female, with her stocky, elongated body, often beautifully marked in silver, black and yellow, can usually be seen sitting head downwards in the centre of her broad web and the minute brown male, which may also accompany her, scarcely seems at first sight to bear any relationship at all to the giant female. The female of the American *Nephila clavipes* weighs in at around one hundred males, while some tropical species have females weighing nearly one thousand times as much as the males. This size relationship in *Nephila* can be appreciated by examining Plate 4.2, which

58

Plate 4.2. *Nephila clavipes*. The tiny male is here trying to mate with the huge female, who completely ignores him. Panama.

shows the male and female of a species from Panama together in the web. This enormous disparity in size between the sexes would appear at first to put the puny male in great peril of his life when he approaches his gigantic partner in courtship. The reverse is actually the case, his minute size conferring upon the male a similar degree of immunity from her lungeing jaws to that enjoyed by very small insects which fly into her web. Both the male and these small insects are below the minimum size of her normal prey and therefore not worth considering as food, so they are left alone, which of course allows the male spider to get on with the business of mating. As will be explained shortly, most male spiders, especially those about equal in size to their partners, have had to evolve a complex array of visual and tactile signals in order to seduce their mates and avoid the disaster of becoming a meal. It is almost paradoxical, therefore, to think of the minute male *Nephila* crawling around his partner's enormous body with no risk to his life and treated for the most part as if he did not even exist. There is some difference in size between the sexes in other families, notably the Thomisidae, but in no other spiders has it been taken to the extreme observed in *Nephila*.

Sperm Induction

Since there is no physical connection between the male's testes and the palp with which he introduces the sperm into the female, his first task before setting off in search of a mate is to transfer semen from his genital opening into the spermophores of his palps, a process known as *sperm induction*. Although this does have a parallel with the mating process employed by the dragonflies, it is nevertheless such a strange and remarkable event that the first observations of sperm induction actually taking place were dismissed as unreliable and even false by some arachnologists of the day, who held to the

59

idea that there must be an internal connection between the palps and the testes. It is now recognised as the indispensable first step taken by the male spider in his often strange and fascinating courtship of the female. Although sperm induction obviously takes place extremely often in the wild, it is not an event which many biologists are privileged to witness, except under laboratory conditions, for the observer has to be in the right place at the right time. The act of sperm induction is undertaken in a variety of different ways in different spiders, but in no spiders, not even those with palps long enough to do so, is sperm taken straight from the genital opening. At its simplest, e.g. in *Pholcus*, the daddy-longlegs spider, a single thread is held taut across the genital opening and on it is deposited a single drop of semen. This is picked up in the chelicerae and absorbed by alternate application of the palps.

Among the mygalomorph tarantulas, sperm induction is a process which can take as long as 3 hours. A broad silken sheet is spun, leaving a large oval opening and a second smaller opening, between which lies a narrow band of strong silk. Crawling through the larger of the holes and lying on his back,

Fig. 4.2. *Araneus quadratus*. A male on his sperm web charging his palps from the tiny drop of sperm that he has deposited on it.

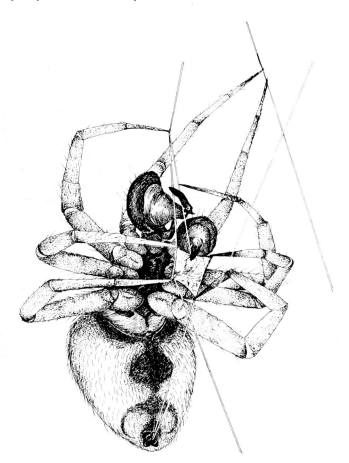

the male rubs the area near his genital opening onto the silk band to strengthen it, then he strokes the genital area and deposits a droplet of sperm onto the underside. He then climbs back and sits above the droplet, reaching around the edge of the reinforced band to absorb the sperm by rhythmically tapping his palps alternately into it.

In most spiders, the process is accomplished far more quickly and with a considerably less elaborate sperm web. The male of the European orb web spider, *Araneus quadratus*, in common with many other species, first constructs a neat, triangular little web, usually attached to nearby grass stems. He deposits a drop of sperm onto the upper surface and then hangs off the edge of the web with his body at right-angles to its upper surface and alternately dips his palps into the droplet (Fig. 4.2), which is completely absorbed within about 10 minutes. He then wanders off in search of a female. It is important to note that the actual presence of a female is not necessary to trigger sperm induction; this is a purely instinctive process, which takes place automatically once the male is mature and then after each mating, a process which is inherited as part of the spider's racial memory. The actual complex courtship behaviour is, however, only carried out when the female is present or when her former presence in a particular spot can be detected by the male.

Courtship

With his palps fully charged with sperm, the male is now ready for courtship and copulation with the female of his species, but this can be a time of great danger for him as his potential mate may not be as interested in mating as he is. Apart from her often considerably larger size, she will have devoted the whole of her life so far to the capturing of prey and feeding. Her instincts, therefore, are very much of a predatory nature and, unless the courting male trespassing in her territory or web can in some way signal to her that he is a male of her species, he will be in imminent danger of ending up as a meal instead of a mate. As a direct consequence of these inherent difficulties, male spiders have evolved an elaborate and amazing variety of courtship rituals, which in certain instances may even rival the displays of the most flamboyant and inventive birds. The form of courtship varies according to the life style of the particular spider and the importance attached to the various senses in its everyday life.

In those species where the web is all important as a sense aid, the silken lines are used by the males to signal their intentions to the female occupants, courtship usually proceeding via a series of tweakings or vibrations of the web by the intruding male, signals which the female should recognise. In the hunting spiders, methods of courtship vary enormously and depend partly upon the quality of eyesight possessed by a particular species. Those having sharp eyesight and therefore capable of resolving detail with some clarity have evolved fairly complex sight-based courtship rituals during which the male uses complicated movements of his legs, palps and body to make his intentions known to the female. The most skilful exponents of this visual courtship are the sharp-sighted little jumping spiders, who perform the most bizarre prenuptial dances. This visual courtship is often assisted by adornments on the male's body, such as tufts of hair on the head and brushes on the legs, the whole effect being reinforced by his colours, which are often of a glittering metallic nature and in contrasting shades.

From this ultimate in visual courtship, there is a series of intergrades, ending in spiders who seem to manage perfectly adequately with almost no courtship at all. The short-sighted hunter falls about mid-way between the two extremes, involving less elaborate displays by the males as the females' eyesight would not be sufficiently acute to distinguish the details of a more elaborate affair. Whatever the method of courtship used, however, the initiative is almost always on the male's part and he alone shoulders the responsibility for ensuring recognition by his prospective mate and seducing her into a state of submission whereupon mating can take place. Also, being a great deal more disposable than the female, the male can be safely exposed to the dangers inherent in wandering around vulnerably in search of her. If an incompetent male does make a mess of courtship by failing to communicate his amorous intentions to the female, then he is likely to end up being her next meal. This is no real loss to the species as a whole, since his body will feed the eggs developing inside the female who will eventually mate with a more successful male.

Spiders can therefore be conveniently divided into three groups for discussion, according to the type of courtship employed. The first of these groups is made up of the short-sighted hunters, most of whom have a rather generalised form of courtship related to their poor sight; the second consists of the long-sighted hunters, who have evolved more specialised and complex displays related to their increased perception of depth and detail, and finally there are the web-builders, with their fine sense of touch, who employ the web as a communication line during courting. Each of these groups will now be considered in more detail by using specific examples from different spider species.

Short-Sighted Hunters

The majority of this group are drably coloured in browns, greys and blacks and spend much of their life on the ground, under stones or under peeling bark, emerging mainly at night to hunt their prey. Information about their immediate surroundings is conveyed to them almost entirely via their taste or touch sense, their legs being used a great deal to test objects around them. It would appear, therefore, that males of these spiders must have an almost insoluble problem in finding the females, with courtship and mating relying on a chance encounter in the dark. That this is patently not the case is evidenced by the abundance of these spiders and it is this abundance which probably contributes to their survival for, at high population densities, the

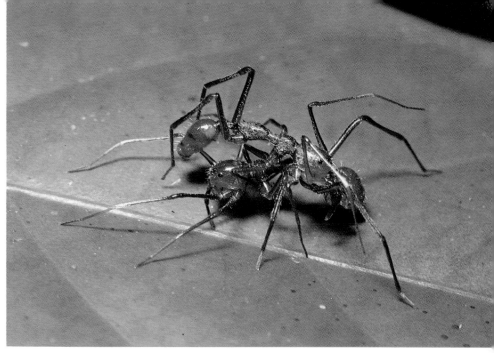

Plate 4.3. *Myrmecium* sp. Originally thought to be a photograph of an ant-mimicking spider catching an ant, a count of legs showed this to be a mating pair of Clubionids. Trinidad.

Plate 4.4. *Thomisus onustus*. The beautiful pink female crab spider is seen here during mating; the tiny male can just be seen under her abdomen. Europe.

chances of males and females meeting by accident are greatly increased. This cannot be the complete answer for, if the population were to fall drastically, e.g. following a hard winter, then males would be much less likely to meet females and the population might continue to fall to extinction. It seems certain, therefore, that another sense is involved to help the males find the females and it is probable that, as in insects, the female emits a chemical attractant, called a *pheromone*, to which the male responds. Some proof for this idea comes from Australia, where male funnel web mygalomorph spiders, *Atrax infensus*, have been attracted to traps merely by using an enclosed female as bait. The actual presence of the female is not even required, for the scent which she has left behind her will often attract a male to the spot, where he may even go through a complete courtship ritual to a non-existent audience. Male trapdoor spiders are probably guided to the female's burrow by an attractant pheromone in the first instance, where they then come into contact with her silk, which may have been left as a webbing around the burrow entrance or may be left from a previous prey capture. This recognition of the female's silk is extremely important in the male's location of the female and is a feature of all spiders.

In the mygalomorphs and some simpler true spiders, the female lacks an epigyne and the male possesses a simple palp. In these spiders, courtship is at its least complex and is almost all done by touch. The courtship of the American mygalomorph tarantula, *Dugesiella hentzii*, for example, is trig-gered once the male on his wanderings comes into contact with the female's body, on which he beats a rapid tattoo with his front legs as the first step in his seduction of her, manoeuvring as he does so to face her. Her first reaction to his unexpected assault is to raise her front legs in her characteristic posture of threat and defence. (This posture is similar in most mygalomorphs and is shown in Plate 3.1). The tapping and stroking actions now adopted by the male modify this behaviour into a state of supplication and she rises high on her hind legs, while at the same time maintaining her basic defence posture. As a final act of submission to the male's advances, she opens her fangs, which are caught and held by special hooks provided for just this purpose on the front legs of the male. This acts as a safeguard against possible injury or death while copulation takes place, perhaps because the female may 'forget' what is going on and may take an unexpected and probably fatal bite at her suitor. The posture adopted also aids in the actual mating, allowing the male to force back the female's cephalothorax while drumming with his palps on her sternum. After the short mating, which lasts only a minute or so, the male leaves, usually unhindered by any menacing lunges on the part of the female.

The small, drab brown species of *Clubiona* are found in both Europe and the USA and have no particular courtship at all, the male merely roughly grabbing hold of the female and mating with her, although he must be careful not to let go once he has found her (Plate 4.3). The two sexes of the Gnaphosids, *Drassodes* and *Zelotes*, live in silken cells, often close to one another, under stones or peeling bark. The male matures earlier than the female and mates with her just after her final moult, when she is mature but in no fit state to resist his advances, because her new exoskeleton has not yet hardened and her jaws are ineffective. The male may even stake his claim to an immature female by moving in with her and sharing her cell until she reaches maturity, or by building his own cell right next to hers. In another Gnaphosid, the European mouse spider, *Herpyllus blackwalli* (so-called because it resembles a miniature grey mouse scuttling around in human habitations — its normal habitat), the males are very similar in both appearance and size to the females. A meeting between the two is the signal for some fierce sparring accompanied by a violent jerking of the body. Real courtship, however, seems to be lacking and the death of either participant may be the result but a receptive female will simply give up her part of the contest and permit the male to crawl over her and mate.

A somewhat different type of behaviour is to be found in the beautiful green Sparassid, *Micrommata virescens*, a species fairly common in Europe and widely, although extremely locally, distributed in England. The mature male is a handsome spider, slim and elegant with a bright yellow abdomen with green flanks with three contrasting red bands down its length. The first encounter between the male and female *Micrommata* is somewhat rough and ready, the male jumping straight at her without any kind of preliminary courtship and unceremoniously grabbing her leg or abdomen in his chelicerae. Despite her great size advantage over the male, the female reacts in an amazingly subdued manner, giving no resistance and simply allowing the male to climb onto her back and, caressing her with his legs, to lean across and insert one of his palps into her epigyne.

Many of the Misumenoid crab spiders normally to be found sitting around in flowers or on leaves also exhibit few of the introductory gestures associated with courtship in the true sense. In many species, the male is considerably smaller than the female and a great deal more agile. The diminutive orange-brown male of the European *Thomisus onustus* merely climbs on to the broad, humped back of his beautiful pink mate (Plate 4.4), tickles and caresses her and mates with her at his will while she remains completely passive. The male of the far more common *Misumena vatia* behaves in much the same way, walking straight on to the female who seems to ignore him completely.

Pride of place for originality in courtship amongst the short-sighted hunters, however, must surely go to the long-legged males of the *Xysticus* crab spiders. The strange nuptial behaviour of these spiders was first observed in the very common European *Xysticus cristatus*. The techniques employed were so strange that they elicited a great deal of disbelieving comment at the time, until subsequent observations in other countries proved the case to be beyond doubt.

The male *Xysticus cristatus* is smaller and darker than the female and has much longer front legs. Immediately upon meeting a female, he grasps one of her front legs by its femur. This unexpected attack normally provokes a short scuffle, during which he holds on to his advantage and then crawls onto her

Plate 4.5. *Xysticus cristatus*. Here the male crab spider is in the process of tying down his mate with strands of silk. Europe.

Plate 4.6. *Xysticus cristatus*. Having tied down the female with silk strands, which show up clearly over her cephalothorax, the male now proceeds to mate with her.

back, circling round and gently stroking her with his legs. This gentle fondling is common to many spiders and helps to put the female into a submissive frame of mind, but in *Xysticus* it has an additional more concrete purpose for, as he circles over and around her, he leaves a silken thread behind him which ties her down by her head and legs to whatever she is sitting on. This tiny web has been called the *bridal veil* and only when it is complete does the male gently lift his mate's abdomen upwards from the rear and crawl head first underneath it. While in this position, mating takes place, an act which may take 90 minutes, during which time the female does not attempt to break free from her bonds. Only after the male has left her does she disentangle herself from the veil of threads, which has served its purpose by preventing her seizing the male at the vulnerable instant of his departure. The spinning of this bridal veil (Plates 4.5 & 6) is undoubtedly one of the most unusual and amazing habits displayed by spiders and, added to their numerous other bizarre activities, it is small wonder that their devotees seldom become bored and blasé about their subjects.

Long-Sighted Hunters

The hunters in this group actively hunt their prey by day and this diurnal habit enables courtship to take place in conditions where both attitudes of display and bright colour or modified outgrowths can be perceived and their purpose interpreted to best effect. There is a certain parallel to the spider situation in Lepidopteran insects, with the short-sighted hunters above being represented by the rather drab night-flying moths and the long-sighted hunters being represented by those supremely diurnal insects, the butterflies, who court and mate under the sun, often using their bright colours, as well as scent, to establish identity in their sexual encounters. Of the spiders included here, several have received appropriate common names to fit their active habits, such as jumping spider, lynx spider and wolf spider.

In a number of the common *Pardosa* wolf spiders, a male will commence courtship of a female who is still several centimetres away and who has not been contacted at all by touch, as is necessary in the previous group. Here, courtship is triggered solely by the sight of the female, but it can probably also be stimulated by pheromones or by a combination of both visual and scent signals. The idea that pheromones are involved is reinforced by the observation that males of *Pardosa amentata* will advance with full courtship display towards a spot recently vacated by a female of the species, the inference being that she has left her scent behind her. The purpose of the male's display is twofold, firstly to induce recognition of his presence and acceptance of his advances and secondly, by varying the details of the courtship dance, to prevent mating taking place between closely related species. This may be especially important in the *Pardosa* spiders, for several species can occur together in quite substantial numbers in the same habitat, with frequent encounters between males and females of species which are different but may closely resemble each other. Males, especially among some insects, may often attempt courtship, and sometimes even mating, with females of another species, but should this occur in the spiders then the likelihood of such an attempt being followed through to mating is very remote, for the females are conditioned to respond receptively only to a male whose display agrees exactly with that of the male of her own species. Should the male eventually come into contact with a female of the wrong species, then her taste and scent will immediately inform him that things are not right and that mating should not be attempted, although, even if it was, the unique structure of the palp and epigyne of each species should prevent mating from being successful.

Most male wolf spiders have the palps and front legs furnished with an ornamentation of some sort, most often consisting of jet-black hairs on the palps, sometimes accompanied by sharply contrasting white marks, which help to make them extremely conspicuous as they are waved around during courtship. Larger species of *Lycosa* usually have darker front legs which may bear black tufts of hairs.

In Europe, it is easy to locate courting couples of the common and very widespread *Pardosa amentata*, for they are found in a wide range of habitats, including gardens, where they will seek out a sunny spot on piles of wood or bare patches of earth. Not only will the males be found courting receptive females, but they will also court females who have already been fertilised and are swollen with eggs, wasting their time in so doing, because the females totally ignore them. The male is slightly smaller than the female, with a slimmer abdomen and longer legs, making him on the whole more agile. In this species, the sooty black palps of the male are a conspicuous adornment and play a major role in the courtship procedures (Fig. 4.3). Upon spotting a female sunning herself, perhaps three or four centimetres away, the male stops abruptly, then, raising himself high on his legs, he stretches his palps out on either side, holding one up at an angle of 45° and holding the other downwards at the same angle, like a human being using semaphore. Maintaining this attitude, he quivers his palps and front pair of legs and

Fig. 4.3. *Pardosa amentata*. The male wolf spider on the right can be seen waving his palps, signalling his good intentions to the female as he approaches her. Europe.

sometimes also his abdomen. Gradually he advances in a jerky fashion towards the female, repeating his semaphore signals over and over again, occasionally rapidly vibrating his front legs. Next he reverses the position of his palps, lowering one and raising the other. If the female is unreceptive to these apparently amusing antics, she will lunge forward and drive him off, his long legs then carrying him safely away from her open fangs, but within seconds he will be before her again, doggedly performing his display again and again, no matter how unwilling she is to receive him. If, however, she is in a receptive mood, his performance will have the desired effect and she will show her acceptance of him by vibrating her front legs.

Both *Pardosa nigriceps* and *Pardosa lugubris* commonly associate with the above species but show distinct differences in their courtship procedures. The male *Pardosa nigriceps* jerkily rotates his especially large black palps in an action best likened to that of feet on the pedals of a bicycle. In addition, he alternately raises and stretches one of his front legs towards the female. The male *Pardosa lugubris*, on the other hand, sits high on his legs, stretching the first pair horizontally outwards on either side. In this posture, he abruptly raises just one black palp vertically with a rather jerky action, pausing briefly before raising the other to the same position and posing for a moment. Finally, he gently vibrates his front legs up and down while lowering his palps to their normal position, repeating the above sequence until he can touch the female. A similar variety of actions has also been observed in the American species of *Pardosa*, each differing significantly from the other and from those of the European species.

In the USA, many Lycosid species have been found to use a form of acoustic communication generated by stridulatory devices on the male palps; these produce sounds inaudible to us but not to the female, an important factor for species which perform their courtship at night. One American species, however, *Lycosa gulosa*, has a parallel in the European buzzing spider and was once called the purring spider from the way the male taps his palps and abdomen against dry leaves, producing a sound probably audible to the female but also to man.

The Pisaurid wolf spider, *Pisaura mirabilis*, from Europe, has taken an original and effective step forward in the proceedings leading up to mating. First he catches a fly or other insect but, rather than following the usual procedure of feeding on it, he stands on tiptoe and wraps the insect in an encircling weft of threads. In a state of great excitement, he now walks jerkily in search of a female, carrying his juicy parcel held firmly in his chelicerae. Upon discovering a female, he takes up a very odd pose before her, angling his body vertically downwards with the tip of his abdomen resting on the ground and the first pair of legs held upwards with the tips of their femurs touching just above his head, while both palps are held upwards and out towards either side. This has the effect of positioning the insect parcel between himself and the female. If the female is receptive to his advances, she approaches him, whereupon he gradually leans over backwards lifting the fly tantalisingly upwards. Then, as she cranes upwards to grasp the fly in her chelicerae, he rapidly alters his position, swivelling round to place his head underneath her sternum. With his mate now busy feeding on the fly, the male crouches, facing towards the rear of her body in a nearly inverted position and mating proceeds. That the fly is vital in inducing the female to mate rather than attack has been established by placing a male lacking a gift into a cage containing a female, whereupon she proceeded to eat him. Sometimes the male plays a duplicitous role by enshrouding the empty husk of a fly, or by trotting off with the gift after the mating is completed.

It has already been said that pride of place for bright colouration and extrovert antics during courtship is held by the jumping spiders, those charming and perky little creatures with their huge, glistening orbs of front eyes, which gaze back at the observer with every indication of intelligence and perception. Many tropical species are fairly large and often brilliantly coloured in reds, blues, greens, mauves, purples, yellows and silver, often with an overall metallic sheen reminiscent of the scales of some butterflies. This brilliance is characteristic of the males, the females being usually clad in somewhat more sombre hues. The chelicerae of the males may be considerably enlarged, oddly shaped and brightly coloured, while their faces may be adorned with crests or plumes of hairs. The front legs are long and beautifully ornamented with a variety of enlarged areas, in bright colours, and can bear fringes of long, coloured hairs, scales and enlarged spines.

Though generally less gaudy and rather smaller than some of their tropical relatives, the jumping spiders of the USA are nevertheless often remarkably beautiful and strikingly coloured, especially members of the genus *Phidippus*, e.g. the bright orange *Phidippus apacheanus* whose female rivals the male in beauty. Their front legs are very attractive, with long fringes of coloured hairs, while the face is adorned with tufts of hairs and coloured bands of hairs and scales. Some *Phidippus* males wave their front legs with such enthusiasm that they cross at the tips but more usually they are held up at about 45° to reveal the plumes and coloured areas as they zig-zag their way towards the females.

The British jumping spiders are all rather small and, although lacking bright colours, their patterns are often quite striking and pleasing to the eye. One of the more commonly encountered species is *Euophrys frontalis*, whose courting males and females can be found near or on the ground amongst stones and grass. The female is pale yellow-brown in colour, with darker markings consisting of rows of blotches on the abdomen and she attains a maximum length of 5 mm ($\frac{3}{16}$ in). The male is smaller and darker; the head is deep black and, like the carapace, is clothed with black and white hairs. The metatarsi of the front legs are black and the colour gradually pales to olive green on succeeding segments to the coxa; in contrast to this, the tarsi are white and covered in long white hairs, while the anterior eyes are fringed with vivid orange hairs. The palps also show sharp contrasts between the segments, the femurs being dark brown to black, with the other segments yellow-brown; the inner and upper surfaces of the patella and tibia are clothed with white hairs. Upon confronting a female, the male raises his attractive front legs into an almost vertical position and then raises himself higher on the rest of his legs as courtship proceeds (Fig. 4.4). Snapping his

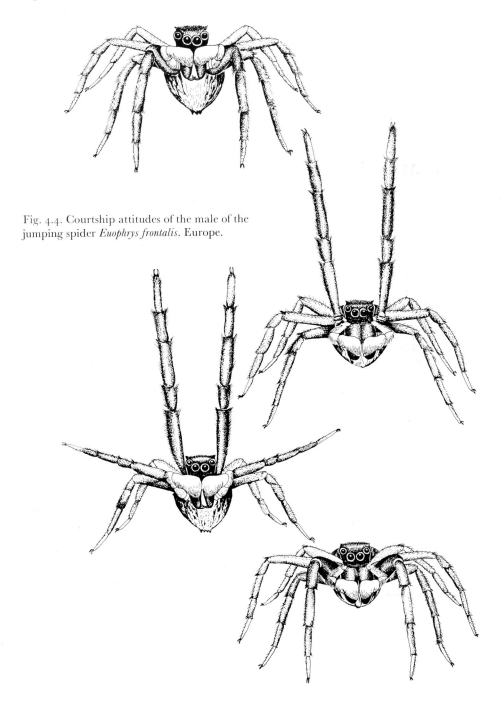

Fig. 4.4. Courtship attitudes of the male of the jumping spider *Euophrys frontalis*. Europe.

front legs upwards and jerking his body, he moves forward a step at a time towards the female, constantly vibrating his palps with their conspicuous white fringes, above which peer his huge front eyes with their brilliantly coloured fringe of hairs. So mesmeric is his display that the female cannot tear her gaze from his advancing form, even if she is unreceptive to his advances. By jerking her body up and down she can signal rejection but, if acceptance is more her mood, then she allows him to crawl delicately over her and insert his palp into the epigyne.

Occasionally, two male jumping spiders will meet face to face and the sight of each other is often sufficient to trigger a courtship display in both of them. There is, however, no actual attempt to mate and, as the two meet head-on, they adopt a curious attitude, each with his fangs clearly bared and pressed against those of his rival, while the delicate palps are held backwards out of harm's way. Whether this behaviour can be interpreted as an example of mistaken courtship or male rivalry is difficult to say, but a challenge of the kind described between two males of an Australian species is depicted in Fig. 4.5 below.

Fig. 4.5. *Helpis minitabunda.* Two male jumping spiders sparring with each other, fangs bared. Australia.

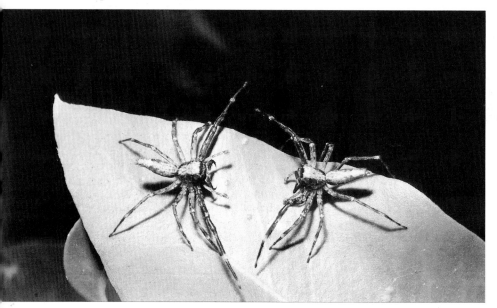

Web-Building Spiders

The spiders in this group mostly have very small eyes incapable of rendering an accurate or detailed picture of the outside world. Instead they have come to rely almost completely on their acute touch sense, extending this beyond the span of their eight legs to encompass the whole radius of their webs, which serve to transmit information back to them. The senses of these spiders are finely tuned to detect the vibrations caused by any interloper in the web, vibrations which result in the occupant of the web racing across to the area of disturbance. If, of course, the interloper happens to be suitable prey then it will be wrapped up and consumed at the spider's convenience.

When the males of these spiders trot off in search of a mate, they are eventually forced to enter into the home of a female, who has so far devoted her life to killing anything which sets up vibrations in her web. Ascertaining whether or not the web belongs to a female of his own species is not difficult for the male spider, because he can recognise her silk, probably by its distinctive taste or smell. His problem, once he has found her web, is to inform the aggressive occupant, who is usually bigger than he is, that she should react to his trespass by submitting to him rather than by wrapping and eating him. His method of overcoming this problem is logical enough for it uses the tactile senses so efficiently utilised by the female and, by tweaking the web in a regular and rhythmic manner, he is able to transmit to her a code informing her of his presence and his nature. That his signalling should be regular is of vital importance, for an insect blundering into the web will send totally random vibrations, with the inevitable result, whereas the regular signals of the male usually elicit a different and much less vigorous response. The male does not trust completely the submission of the female and always takes care to trail a life-line of silk behind him, ready to swing down to safety instantly if the female attacks. He is in fact extremely adept at avoiding her attacks, his smaller size being an asset, and it is only on rare occasions that his courtship, whether or not successfully concluded, results in his death at the hands of his mate. This is somewhat contrary to the views expressed in less well informed literature.

Some of the web-builders do not fit easily into this group and are more akin to the long-sighted hunters in their courtship and mating behaviour. In the European *Agelena labyrinthica*, whose flat sheet webs may be common and conspicuous objects amongst grass and other low vegetation, the long-legged male is almost as large as the female and announces his arrival in her web by tapping with his palps as he walks towards her. The results of his signals may be somewhat surprising for, if she is in a receptive frame of mind, she immediately draws in her legs and collapses as if paralysed. In this condition she allows herself to be manhandled in a way typical of the Agelenidae and he drags her off to any place that he considers suitable for mating, sometimes near the edge of the web but more often at the entrance to her funnel (Plate 4.7). The closely related *Agelenopsis pennsylvanica* from the USA behaves in a similar manner.

The European Theridiid, *Steatoda bipunctata*, is common in and around human habitations, particularly in sheds and outhouses and around window frames and it is now well established and spreading in the USA. The female

Plate 4.7. *Agelena labyrinthica*. Male mating with the female at the entrance to the funnel-shaped retreat in her web. Europe.

reaches about 7 mm (just over $\frac{1}{4}$ in) in length and is immediately re-cognisable by her shiny brown abdomen with its paler brown markings. The slightly smaller male has large palps and initiates his courtship of the female by walking jerkily around in her web while at the same time twitching his abdomen up and down. A receptive female responds to this by plucking at the web to guide the mate to her, but he only approaches her after he has walked up and down, using silk to construct a special bridge where mating will take place. With vibrating legs, he entices her onto this bridge where she hangs slightly downwards to allow him to mate with her.

Courtship in the European garden spider and in a number of other *Araneus* species is considerably less good-natured than in *Steatoda* and, in fact, it can be quite a trying experience to observe it. The female garden spider can be a large and fearsome creature up to 12 mm ($\frac{1}{2}$ in) in length, twice the length of the male and she is considerably heavier. So, with the utmost stealth, the male creeps unnoticed into her web until he reaches the topmost strand, then very gently he begins tweaking at the silk (Plate 4.8), dodging her immediate headlong rush at him by swinging agilely down on his silken life-line. Persistence, however, is his trademark and he clambers up again and again onto her web, the whole performance often being repeated dozens of times as the male tirelessly and doggedly sticks to his task. Like most Araneidae, he makes his task more difficult by producing a special mating thread and she must be lured onto this by a series of tugs and jerks. Finally, if the female has not already mated, she will succumb to his persistent seduction, showing her submission by holding her head downwards. Frequently, the female will already have mated and then the little male's tireless activity will be fruitless,

74

Plate 4.8. *Araneus quadratus*. the male (right) can be seen tweaking the web with his front leg as he signals his approach to his potentially dangerous mate. Europe.

for if he makes a single mistake he will be lucky to escape with his life.

It is strange that such a tedious and dangerous courtship has evolved in the garden spider and in other spiders of the genus *Araneus*, because other species within the Araneidae do things in a much more civilised and less energetic manner. The male and female of *Meta segmentata* from Europe often co-exist quite happily in the female's web for some time before actual courtship and mating take place. This apparently harmonious relationship is probably only possible because the male is as big and powerful as his mate and has much longer front legs, giving him an immediate advantage when any sparring takes place. In spring, and again in autumn, practically every web, which for identification purposes has an open, circular area in the centre of the orb, contains both a male and female, neither showing any signs of life or the slightest interest in each other until the arrival of a third party signals the moment for courtship to begin. As an insect flies into the web, the female runs down to bite and wrap it. The male, meanwhile, reacts in a more leisurely way, gradually approaching the insect which the female is busy subduing. Putting the insect between himself and the female, the male gradually advances (Fig. 4.6), gently tweaking the web with little jerks of his abdomen, then reaching forward with his long front legs he gently tickles the female. Her response is to retreat, leaving the fly in his possession. He may show a certain amount of interest in the insect, perhaps biting it briefly, but in reality he is only using it to further the cause of his courtship. Normally, she soon returns to her meal and he again resumes his stroking but, if she fails to return after a short period of time, he lures her back to the insect by gently pulling on the web. Now, walking backwards and forwards over her, he

Fig. 4.6. *Meta segmentata*. The courting male on the left approaches the female while she is busily engaged in feeding on a fly. Europe.

constructs a mating web onto·which he must lure her. Sometimes he may even begin to wrap a few threads of silk around her body, as if his predatory instincts were beginning to override his sexual desires, but she always frees herself eventually. Courtship may continue for a fairly lengthy period and sometimes a female will retreat to her lair and leave the unfortunate male in sole possession of the insect, but a receptive mate will finally be enticed onto the mating web, where she hangs in a horizontal pose for mating to take place.

On both sides of the Atlantic are found various members of the genus *Tetragnatha*, the grass spiders or big-jawed spiders, apt names for these slim-bodied spiders with their enlarged chelicerae. Typical of them is *Tetragnatha extensa*, commonly found in Britain in damp grassy places, such as marshes and the margins of lakes, ponds and rivers, where their characteristic horizontally placed orb webs may be quite common. The male's chelicerae are even longer than those of the female and, in addition, they have a strong spur which juts out from near the top of the basal section, this spur showing up clearly in Fig. 4.7. As with the majority of spiders, a special adornment present in the male alone is likely to have some role in courtship and this is certainly the case with the cheliceral spur. The male, with chelicerae gaping wide, walks boldly into the female's rather scrappy web, whereupon she comes to meet him with her chelicerae likewise fully open. As they meet, their front legs touch and the male uses his own legs to push those of the female out of the way at right angles on either side of her body. Now her front end is fully accessible and their chelicerae meet, the female's slipping neatly behind the male's spurs where they are firmly held, preventing her from attempting to bite him (Fig. 4.7). At the same time, a second spur projecting from the inner edge of the male's chelicerae provides additional security, while the male's

Fig. 4.7. *Tetragnatha extensa*. The way in which the jaws of the male and female of the members of the Tetragnathidae lock together during mating shows up clearly here. Europe and USA.

long fangs are curled around those of the female to complete the secure grip which he now has on her and which prevents her from attacking him during the vulnerable period of mating. With the female held in this position, they move into a vertical stance, heads downwards and with their bellies facing (Plate 4.9), while the male's long palps bridge the gap between them and are inserted into the female's epigyne. *Tetragnatha* females seem very ready to offer their fangs to the male's grip and frequently seem as ready to mate as he is, although unreceptive or previously mated females will ferociously drive off any intruding males. Occasionally two males will be seen circling a single female at the same time, as she makes desperate lunges in all directions in an attempt to drive them off.

It has already been said that the males of *Nephila* owe their immunity to

Plate 4.9. *Tetragnatha extensa*. In this side view of a mating pair, the inflated palp of the male can be seen being inserted into the underside of the female's abdomen. Europe and USA.

attack by the female to their small size and the males of the Araneid genus *Argiope* are also very much smaller than the females. The large orange females of the American *Argiope aurantia* frequently have three or four of these pygmy males in attendance on the outskirts of the web and, as with *Araneus*, they conduct their courtship by tweaking and vibrating the web. Males approaching from behind are often allowed to creep over the female's body, her normal reaction merely being to brush them off with one of her legs and only males showing a high degree of persistence will eventually mate.

The web-building money spiders of the family Linyphiidae are rather small for observations on their courtship but, needless to say, details of some of them have been recorded. Under the microscope, a number of males in particular can be seen to be furnished with strange grooves, lobes and turrets on their heads, which give them a quite extraordinary appearance and which would certainly make them of considerable interest to more spider buffs if only they were visible to the naked eye. (A selection of these males is shown in Fig. 2.2.) Since the females lack these adornments, it is almost certain that they have been developed to assist in some way with courtship and mating and the grooves in the head of the male of at least one species have been seen to be gripped by the female during mating.

One point worth making is that male spiders do not seek out females on every day within a given period, or even for the whole of a single day, for even when males mature they will not venture forth in search of a mate unless the weather conditions are right. Warm, still, humid evenings in England seem to be very favourable for many spiders and, at such a time, as many as a dozen pairs of *Tetragnatha extensa* may be found mating within a relatively small area, whereas in the same place a day later, in cooler, windier conditions, no mating pairs will be found.

Mating Process

It can clearly be seen from the above account that male spiders frequently have to go to a great deal of trouble to seduce the females into a state where they will allow mating to take place. However aggressive she may have been to the initial approach of the male, and no matter how long the courtship involved in her seduction, once she has acquiesced, the female falls into a kind of trance until mating is completed. With all those legs sticking out in all directions, a certain amount of care needs to be taken to assume a position where efficient transfer of sperm from male palp to female epigyne can take place and two principal postures are adopted to facilitate this procedure. In the mygalomorphs, the six-eyed spiders and the web-builders, the male uses a frontal approach and moves underneath the female's sternum, where he can apply his palps directly. This position is particularly advantageous in the web-builders for the female hangs head down below the male in a position where her potential to menace him is greatly reduced and his retreat after mating can safely be made before she realises what has happened and can make any move to catch him. This position is less satisfactory for the male of the wandering spiders, for he is positioned directly beneath the female's menacing jaws and his retreat, once mating is complete and her ardour is dampened, involves considerable danger. After mating, therefore, he leaps away from the female immediately and with great agility.

The second mating position is adopted by the more active spiders, such as the wolf spiders and jumping spiders. Here the male crawls over the female's body with his head pointing towards the rear of her abdomen, from which position he reaches round the side of her body and applies a single palp to her epigyne. There is little danger to the male in this position and, indeed, the females often ignore his presence completely and may sometimes awaken sufficiently from their trance to run around with the male still in position, mating sometimes taking an hour. He may change the palps often, entering the epigyne with each in turn. In some of the ambushing spiders, such as *Thomisus onustus* and *Misumena vatia*, the broad bodies of the females so dwarf the males that the latter are forced to adopt a special posture in which they cling beneath the abdomen in order to reach the epigyne with their palps.

The length of time required to complete the transfer of sperm and the number of times the palps are inserted varies enormously from species to species. As far as some of the species already described under Courtship are concerned, *Micrommata* mating is a long drawn-out process which can last as

79

long as 6 or 7 hours, with each palp being inserted once. In *Steatoda*, the male inserts each palp once for a lengthy period, perhaps as much as 2 hours, and, in the interval between changing from one palp to the other, he leaves the female and chews his palps, later resuming mating. Resumption of mating does, however, require a bout of stridulatory movements of the abdomen from the male, using the apparatus described earlier. The ability of *Steatoda* to break off and leave the female during mating and then to return with the minimum of fuss is no doubt in large part due to the lack of hostility shown by many Theridiid females to their males, who may even be actively encouraged in their task. The male garden spider on the other hand inserts a single palp for about 15 seconds before leaving his hard-won mate, further courtship being necessary before the second palp can be inserted. In extreme cases, mating may take but a few seconds, this being sufficient time for the transfer of adequate sperm to ensure fertilisation of the eggs.

Although a brief description of the structure and working of the palp and epigyne at their simplest was given earlier (p. 32), it is worth adding a few more points of interest about them at this juncture. The complexity of the male palp in many spiders and the corresponding complexity of the matching female epigyne can be likened in a way to a lock and key. The palp represents a key and the epigyne a lock and, as with keys and locks, the wrong key will not open the lock. This means that an effective barrier exists to prevent copulation between spiders of different species for, in all but a few instances, palps and epigynes of these spiders do not fit each other.

Most spiders are polygamous, i.e. they take several mates, some spiders extremely so. Even the females may mate more than once, sometimes after the eggs have been laid. More often though, the female spiders aggressively resist the advances of all but the first one or two of her suitors. Males on the other hand will roam around and mate with every female willing to receive them, although with each successive mating their peril grows for, with age, the male spider gradually loses his agility and is more likely to fall victim to the female's predatory instincts. Further mating in spiders is sometimes prevented by plugs within the epigyne. In *Peucetia viridans*, the green lynx spider from the USA, a hard blackish layer, probably consisting of dried semen, often with the addition of a piece of the male palp, effectively blocks the epigyne, preventing any further attempts at mating.

Chapter 5

Life History of Spiders

In the previous chapter, the reader will have gained an insight into the complicated and unusual courtship and mating procedures employed by the spiders. A convenient point, therefore, to commence a description of the life history of spiders is with the actual laying of the eggs, which eventually follows mating. The production of eggs may in fact be delayed for a considerable time after mating has taken place and, to this end, sperm is stored inside the spermathecae in the female's abdomen. Not all spiders, however, need to mate before eggs can be laid since, in a few species, females only have been discovered. Animals such as these, where the role of the male has become redundant, are described as *parthenogenetic*. For those readers unfamiliar with this phenomenon, it is employed by female aphids, whose unfertilised eggs produce large numbers of offspring in rapid succession during the summer months, permitting a large increase in population in a relatively short time. The advantage to these spiders in being parthenogenetic is probably the lack of complication involved in a life style where there is no requirement to find a mate, an operation which normally takes a great deal of time and energy.

Egg-Laying

As with virtually all aspects of the spider's life, silk is used by the female during egg-laying, but to a greater or lesser degree depending upon the species concerned. In most spiders, a disc of silk is made upon which the eggs are deposited, accompanied by fluid from the spermathecae containing, of course, the sperm received earlier from the male during mating. It is not until this time, while the eggs are still soft, that actual fertilisation takes place. The outer layer of the egg gradually hardens to provide protection for the delicate contents, the greatest danger at this time being that of desiccation. The female spider then proceeds to envelop the newly laid eggs in further layers of protective silk to form an egg-sac, which is characteristic for a particular species (see below).

The number and size of the eggs laid by different spider species seems to vary with the size of the individual concerned. Generally speaking, small spiders tend to lay very small eggs, often few in number, while larger spiders lay larger numbers of bigger eggs. *Oonops domesticus* for example, a tiny pinkish spider no more than 2 mm (just over $\frac{1}{16}$ in) long, often seen darting around on the walls of houses in Europe, lays only two eggs at a time, whereas some of the world's largest spiders, such as some of the big mygalomorphs, may produce as many as 3000 eggs in a single batch. As for size, the eggs of *Oonops* are only a fraction of a millimetre in diameter, but those of the large mygalomorphs may be as big as a small pea and the newly hatched spiderling may be considerably bigger than the adult *Oonops*. Not all of the eggs are laid at one time and many spiders lay several batches, the general rule seeming to be that the fewer the eggs produced per batch, the larger the number of batches laid. There is also a tendency for the numbers of eggs to fall with each succeeding batch, as the female begins to age; also the supply of sperm available for further batches begins to run short, so that some of the eggs laid fail to become fertilised. In some temperate spiders, the ability to store sperm over considerable periods of time means that egg-sacs may be produced in the autumn of one year and the female then overwinters, proceeding to lay further quantities of eggs in the following spring, without having to mate again in the intervening period. Many of the long-lived female mygalomorphs do, in fact, manage to lay eggs at regular intervals over the whole of their considerable life spans.

Egg-Sac

The newly laid eggs contain the genetic material vital to the continuation of her species and it is not therefore surprising that the female spider often goes to a great deal of trouble to protect the sac and its contents from possible threats. The egg-sacs themselves vary considerably in their final form and in the degree of caring treatment they receive from the female. Generally speaking, the more highly evolved the species of spider, the greater the quantity of protective silk applied to the egg-sac. In more primitive species, such as *Pholcus*, the cosmopolitan daddy-longlegs spider, the eggs are merely held loosely together with a few strands of silk and are then carried in the female's jaws until they hatch. In the trapdoor spiders and other mygalomorphs, which lead a mainly subterranean existence, the rather baggy egg-sacs are suspended from the walls of the burrow, where they are protected from climatic extremes and are also physically protected by the female until some time after the young have emerged from the eggs. In their relatively safe surroundings, freed from the pressures exercised by the harsh vagaries of climate and threats from potential predators, the eggs of these spiders tend to develop more slowly than those of the more advanced free-living spiders.

The practice of retaining and guarding the egg-sac or sacs by the female is common to spiders of many different families (Plate 5.1). Perhaps the most familiar exponents of this habit are the wolf spiders. Several species of small wolf spider belonging to the genus *Pardosa* are common in a variety of habitats, including suburban gardens, and serve well to illustrate the complete process from egg-laying through to hatching of the young.

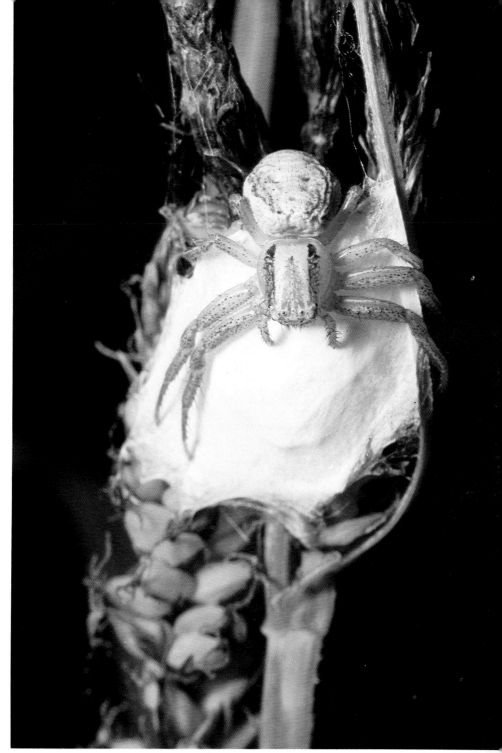

Plate 5.1. *Xysticus cristatus*. A female crab spider guarding her egg-sac. Europe.

The female *Pardosa* first attaches silken lines to surrounding objects to act as a scaffold. Onto this, she proceeds to spin a disc of silk about as broad as her body is long. The closely woven disc is formed as she rotates her body, at the same time sweeping her spinnerets to and fro across the scaffolding, all the while checking the correctness of the diameter by touching the circumference with her palps. This forms the base of the egg-sac and, when complete, it may either be flat or form a shallow dish into which the eggs are laid. A minute or two is all the time required for the actual laying of the eggs. The female stands over the disc with her body in an arched position and extrudes a viscous fluid in which the eggs are laid; the viscosity of the fluid permits the generally globular shape of the egg-mass to be maintained and prevents it flowing off the edge of the disc. The fluid contains the sperm from the male and it is now that fertilisation takes place. When the female has finished laying her eggs, she begins, without changing position, to cover them with their first sheet of protective silk, moving in circles around the disc and raising and lowering her abdomen as the silk streams forth. This completed, she cuts the lens-shaped structure free of its scaffold and proceeds to oversew the seam between top and bottom, holding the sac in her chelicerae, palps and third pair of legs. The whole mass is then revolved and additional silk is added until an almost spherical object is produced. Immediately after completion, *Pardosa* egg-sacs are white but, within a short time, normally a few hours, they have changed to various shades of grey, yellow, blue or green. Having accomplished her task, the female attaches the egg-sac to her spinnerets and carries it faithfully with her at all times until the eggs begin to hatch (Fig. 5.1).

Fig. 5.1. *Pardosa amentata*. A female with her egg-sac sitting on a log in the warmth of the sun. Europe.

In its position beneath the tip of the abdomen, the bulky sac seems to be of little inconvenience to her as she runs unimpeded amongst the vegetation. During this period of their lives, the normally retiring females seem to spend a great deal of time sunbathing on fallen logs or patches of bare earth and quite large numbers may be found together in a particularly favourable spot, scampering off in all directions as one approaches, their retreating forms made more conspicuous by the pale egg-sac which each is carrying. Presumably, the increased warmth from this sunbathing habit speeds up development of the eggs, although strong, direct sunlight tends to be avoided as it would desiccate them. It is a fact that those wolf spiders which lead semi-aquatic lives keep their egg-sacs moist by dipping them into the water.

These water-loving members of the genus *Pirata* produce egg-sacs which remain white after completion, so that the females are particularly conspicuous if they are driven from their hiding places amongst the rushes at the water's edge out on to the open surface of the water. Even here they may take cover, especially if the ubiquitous duckweed forms a mat across the surface of the water, for a female caught out in the open will slide sideways beneath the surface like a boat capsizing, taking her bulky egg-sac with her and hanging beneath the fronds of duckweed. When she feels that the danger has passed, she reappears, none the worse for her underwater experience. Her retreat below the water is often so rapid that at first one thinks she has disappeared by magic into thin air and her subsequent re-emergence a few minutes later may be equally puzzling if her initial submergence was not witnessed.

Female wolf spiders clearly show an admirable degree of devotion to their egg-sacs in the ways outlined above and they will also fight valiantly in their defence if an attempt is made to take the sac away from them. Nevertheless, all of these reactions are purely instinctive and it has been established that, once they have laid their eggs, they develop a powerful urge to carry some roughly spherical object in their spinnerets. Indeed, anything of the correct size and shape will suffice as a substitute and curious experimenters have discovered that the spider will adopt a variety of objects, such as an empty snail shell or even a rabbit-dropping, once she has lost her own egg-sac. In terms of survival, of course, her instinct is perfectly adequate, since natural enemies that would deprive her of her egg-sac without also killing and eating the spider herself probably do not exist in nature and it is only curious human beings, upsetting the normal system with their experiments, who have revealed the spider's ability to take on a substitute egg-sac. Despite the spider's efforts to guard her eggs, there are a few enemies so cunning and insidious that they successfully overcome all of her protective care and attention. As happens so often in the natural world, these enemies belong to those ultimate in successful animals, the insects, and several species of parasitic wasps have been hatched from the egg-sacs of wolf spiders. Creeping up on a fierce, predatory spider, whose normal prey is insects, and staying long enough to lay one's eggs inside the spider's egg-sac would seem to be a foolhardy operation, yet the female wasps apparently manage this with sufficient success to maintain their own population. As will be discussed later (p. 102), certain predatory wasps actually specialise in taking spiders as food for their young.

Spiders belonging to the family Pisauridae also carry their egg-sacs around with them until the young hatch out. The large fishing spiders of the genus *Dolomedes*, in Britain called swamp spiders, lay several batches of eggs during the summer and, for 2 to 3 weeks, the female carries the egg-sac attached to her spinnerets and held firmly in her jaws. Its size and bulk are such that she is forced to walk on tiptoe and the presence of the sac obviously impedes her progress through the rank vegetation of her waterside home to a far greater extent than happens with *Pardosa* and *Pirata* females with their egg-sacs. *Dolomedes* often dips the sac into the water and it has been established that, if she fails to do this, then the eggs become too dry and fail to hatch successfully. Rather smaller than *Dolomedes* is the very common European spider, *Pisaura mirabilis*, which frequents much drier habitats and is often found in abundance in rank grassland and in beds of nettles, where it may often be seen sitting on leaves in full sun. A slim, rather long-legged brown or greyish spider, the female trundles around with her whitish egg-sac (Plate 5.2), which she holds in the same manner as *Dolomedes*. Following a period of cool weather, a frequent occurrence at least in the British Isles, *Pisaura* females will often seek an open spot on a leaf, where they sit in a most odd pose, with their legs drawn into their sides, pushing the front half of their body upwards and exposing as much of the egg-sac as possible to the warmth of the sun (Plate 5.3). Presumably this deliberate airing of the eggs following a spell of bad weather is necessary in order to prevent mould developing on them, as well as providing a rise in temperature to speed up the development of the young spiders.

Plate 5.2. *Pisaura mirabilis*. Since she holds her egg-sac in her jaws, the nursery web spider is unable to catch prey during the time that she is carrying it about with her. Europe.

Plate 5.3. *Pisaura mirabilis*. A female nursery web spider exposing her egg-sac to the sun following a period of cold, damp weather. Europe.

Many other female spiders are more sedentary than the wolf spiders and sit in one place with their egg-sacs until the eggs hatch out, often hiding under leaves or stones as they do so. Others build special lairs in which they secrete both themselves and their precious eggs. The charming little female jumping spider, *Evarcha arcuata*, can, for example, often be seen peeping out from her silken nest set snugly between the leaves of a cross-leaved heath plant (Plate 5.4). In Colombia, female jumping spiders have actually been

Plate 5.4. *Evarcha arcuata*. A female jumping spider peers with apparent curiosity from her lair on a bell-heather flowerhead. Europe.

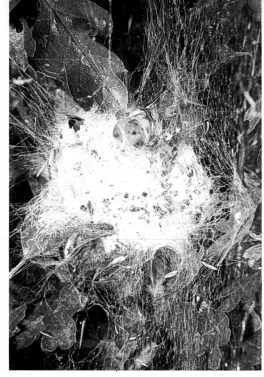

Fig. 5.2. *Agelena labyrinthica*. A view of the complex labyrinth in which the female lays her eggs. The entrance can clearly be seen at the bottom. Europe.

observed actively protecting their eggs from enemies, flicking them away with their long front legs. Even so, some of the eggs were parasitised by wasps, which managed to penetrate the spiders' defences. Many crab spiders construct their egg-sacs out in the open, on grass and other vegetation, the females then clasping them with their legs in a protective embrace, which lasts until they finally die of starvation. The drab little *Xysticus* females may often be found in such circumstances and they will gamely defend their eggs against all-comers, although inevitably various species of parasitic wasp emerge from some of the egg-sacs instead of young crab spiders.

The lengths to which some spiders are prepared to go to protect their eggs and foil the unwelcome attentions of both parasites and predators is beautifully illustrated by *Agelena labyrinthica*, a European sheet web spider. As the name implies, the female builds a large, silken chamber, often in quite a conspicuous spot at the base of a hedge or on a grassy bank, in which there is a series of labyrinthine passages (a view of the outside of the lair is shown in Fig. 5.2). She then places her egg-sacs within the protective maze of silk, which also acts as her own shroud, for she remains there until she dies, guarding her eggs and young. It may be that, by hiding her eggs within this complex of passages, not only does she make it more difficult for a parasite or predator to find them but also makes it more likely that the spider will be able to surprise such an enemy, whose attention is centred entirely upon finding the eggs.

Fig. 5.3. *Agroeca brunnea*. The egg-sac of this species
is covered in a layer of mud which presumably helps
to protect it from predators. Europe.

The egg-sacs of some species may be so conspicuous, at least to human
beings, that they actually draw attention to an otherwise inconspicuous
spider. Such a spider is the Australian *Dichrostichus*, the so-called bolas
spider, which makes several spindle-shaped sacs in a cluster. These are
covered in a very tough outer layer of silk and the female stays with them
until the young hatch. They are referred to as 'cow teats' by Australian
country children on account of their size, shape and colouration.

Not all spiders remain with their eggs, but at least they make some attempt
to ensure their safety, either by laying them in well hidden sites or by
camouflaging them in some way. The sacs may themselves be coloured so
that they blend in with their background or else they may be covered in
pieces of detritus so that they match their surroundings. Females of the genus
Agroeca construct well protected egg-sacs which hang down from a grass stem
like a miniature white bell. Then, during the hours of darkness, the female
laboriously transports mud, in her jaws, up the grass stem and plasters a
layer of it over the silk-covered egg-sac, so that the finished product
resembles a blob of mud adhering to a piece of grass (Fig. 5.3). When dry, the
mud forms a hard protective coat over the eggs, which one would imagine
provides a large measure of security, both by its tough consistency and its
camouflage, but, as with other spiders, several types of parasitic wasp have
been seen to emerge from *Agroeca* egg-sacs. Those spiders, such as some pirate
spiders, which construct an egg-sac similar to that of *Agroeca*, but with a

longer, slimmer stalk, so that it stands well away from the grass stem, and
with no mud covering, appear to rely upon the difficulty any parasite would
have in both finding and gaining access to the structure.

Amongst the lynx spiders, which are frequent elements of the spider fauna
of tropical regions of the world, is found *Peucetia viridans*, a conspicuous and
beautiful species from the southern states of the USA and from Mexico. The
female's egg-sac is a bulky object, much greater in volume than she is and she
hangs head downwards, holding it with her long legs (Plate 5.5). The surface
of the sac is furnished with a number of pointed projections and from these a
number of silken lines normally radiate to nearby leaves. In Mexico, the
spiny pads of the prickly pear cactus and the stinging leaves of the jatropha,
locally called the 'mala mujer' (bad woman), are often chosen by the female
as a site for egg-laying, and the plants themselves may confer some
protection from enemies.

The highly advanced orb web spiders, such as *Araneus* and *Argiope*, have
developed their skills in using silk to a peak of perfection in the construction
of their beautifully intricate webs. It is therefore not surprising to learn that
the egg-sacs of these spiders are especially well provided for in the quantity
and quality of their silk coverings. A number of these spiders incorporate the
sacs into the centre of their webs and some actually use them, along with
other materials, to act as camouflage. Most of them, however, attach the
egg-sacs to some nearby vegetation, either out in the open or under leaves or
flaking bark. The orange *Argiope aurantia* from America hangs her large,

Plate 5.5. *Peucetia* sp. A female lynx spider sitting and protecting her knobbly egg-
sac on a prickly pear cactus pad in Mexico.

pear-shaped egg-sacs close to her web and, in common with close relatives, defies gravity in their production in the following way. She first produces a complex mass of silk and then lays her viscous mass of eggs upwards into this. The hanging yellow ball of eggs is then covered in several sheets of silk of different types and qualities before it is finished off with a yellowish, parchment-like exterior coat. The whole complex process takes several hours of untiring labour and the various types of silk employed give an excellent illustration of the spinning skills of this group of spiders.

The common European garden spider, *Araneus diadematus*, whose plump, gravid female is a familiar sight, sitting head-down in the centre of her dew-covered web in late September, seems to disappear almost overnight towards the end of that month and in early October. Having reached the point in her life when she is full of eggs, she forsakes her web and seeks out some safe place in which to undertake the final act, which will bring her own life to a successful conclusion. Unlike *Argiope*, she chooses a cavity beneath peeling bark or some other concealed place in which to deposit her batch of yellow eggs, numbering between 300 and 800, depending upon her size. She covers the eggs in silk and then sits beside them, waiting out the last remaining days or weeks before the first frosts of winter bring her life to an end.

Development of the Spider

The eggs of spiders contain a large proportion of yolk and the spiderlings which hatch from them are at an advanced stage of development. The subsequent growth and development of the young spiders, through a series of moults, is somewhat akin to that of the less advanced insects, such as the locust, in that the juveniles of both spiders and locusts resemble tiny adults. They have the same general body shape, with a full set of legs, but they lack certain features of the mature adult, such as sexual appendages and, in the locust, wings. In spiders, there is no parallel with the more advanced insects, such as flies and moths, where the larva differs completely from the adult and has to undergo profound changes in the pupal stage.

When the spiderling is ready to emerge, it breaks out of the confines of the egg, aided by an egg tooth. In most species, this newly hatched individual lacks hairs, spines, claws and any colouration and it can neither feed nor produce silk. It has no need of any of these, as it has hatched from the egg mainly to give itself more space to continue development inside the egg-sac, where it now remains, feeding on the ample supplies of yolk which it still has inside its body. Soon it moults for the first time, emerging in a fitter state to cope with the outside world as it is now complete with hairs, spines, claws and colour and can now feed and spin the silk upon which it will depend to a greater or lesser extent for the rest of its life. At this early stage in their lives, spiders, like many other organisms, exhibit certain characteristics derived during the early evolutionary development of their kind and, as a result, spiderlings of many different families resemble one another much more

Fig. 5.4. *Araneus quadratus*. A mass of newly hatched spiderlings. Europe.

closely than they will when they become adult. Having moulted for the first time, the young spiders are still concealed from the outside world within the egg-sac but, when conditions are suitable, they cut their way out and emerge from it. If they are members of a species whose females abandon their eggs, then the newly emerged spiderlings may stay together for a while but eventually they disperse and take up an individual life of their own. Many readers will probably have noticed the centimetre-broad balls of gold and black baby garden spiders (a mass of the closely related *Araneus quadratus* babies is illustrated in Fig. 5.4). These remain intact for several days after hatching, making no attempt to feed, although the warm breath of an inquisitive observer, or even a shadow cast over them as one leans over for a better look, will elicit a mad scramble in all directions, the ball of young gradually reforming after the apparent danger has passed.

Parental Care

Spiders which guard their egg-sacs or carry them around with them may also spend varying amounts of time looking after their newly hatched offspring. Some of the examples already described under Egg-Laying will again suffice to describe the variety of motherly care given to the young. By midsummer, for example, many female *Pardosa* wolf spiders will seem to have suddenly abandoned the egg-sacs which they have been carrying since the late spring and will have assumed a strange hump-backed look. A closer examination will reveal that the humps are actually composed of a mass of baby spiders, which have climbed up onto their mothers' backs after hatching (Fig. 5.5). Apparently the baby wolf spiders are unable to open the tough outer

Fig. 5.5. *Pardosa amentata*. A female wolf spider carrying a mass of newly hatched babies on her back. Europe.

covering of the egg-sac by themselves and rely upon their mother for this important service. She can sense the imminent hatching of her offspring and obliges accordingly by tearing the seam around the sac with her fangs. As many as forty tiny babies may arrange themselves in a neat pile along her abdomen and cling there as she scurries around in search of prey, seemingly unhindered in her movements by the youngsters she is carrying. If they fall off, they quickly remount via their mother's legs or palps, following the silken life-line which they always leave attached to their mother. They do not appear to feed at this time, continuing to survive on the remains of their yolk before undergoing a second moult, which signals the moment when they are to leave their mother and take up an independent existence.

The female Pisauridae have a rather different arrangement for the care of their young. Just before they are due to hatch, the female loosens some of the silk on the outer layers of the egg-sac and attaches the whole structure to some suitable vegetation. Over this, she then weaves a silken tent to form a nursery for the newly emerged young (Plate 5.6). After hatching, the spiderlings cluster in a dark mass, clearly visible to the observer through the silk walls of the tent, protected by the body of their mother, who stands straddling the nest. She will resist a grass stem carefully poked at her but soon abandons her young and retreats into the foliage if something larger threatens. These nursery tents, from which *Pisaura* gets the name nursery web spider, are very noticeable and are often very common in sheltered, grassy areas and, long after the young have dispersed, the nests may still be found, containing now only the empty egg-sac and the cluster of moulted skins left behind by the young spiders.

Amongst members of the Theridiidae, parental care is also fairly often met

Plate 5.6. *Pisaura mirabilis*. A female nursery web spider guards her nest with the egg-sac visible in the centre. Europe.

with. *Enoplognatha ovata* from Europe and North America stands guard over her greyish blue egg-sac, which is usually found enclosed in a curled leaf, although she does not survive to see the emergence of her offspring. Other Theridiids, however, live long enough to care for their family and the most advanced form of parental care is shown by the European species, *Theridion sisyphium*, which, in certain areas, can be a very common spider. The eggs are laid in a spherical, bluish green egg-sac which is hung in a silk-roofed tent in the upper part of the female's web. The newly hatched babies initially feed from liquid which oozes from their mother's mouth and they feed in this way for several days until they are eventually able to share the female's prey (Plate 5.7). She makes their feeding easier by chewing and biting at the prey's (normally an insect's) tough exoskeleton, so that its digesting body contents begin to escape. The young then feed on this liquid in the same way that they previously fed from their mother's mouth. As they increase in size, they even begin to assist their mother in capturing prey by flinging extra strands of silk of their own over the struggling insect.

In some spiders, the young stay with their mother and, when she finally

Plate 5.7. *Theridion sisyphium*. Here the young spiders are sharing a meal, a bee, with their mother. Europe.

dies, having successfully performed her parental duties, they proceed to feed upon her corpse, her final contribution to their welfare. To many people, this may seem sad and grotesque but, in fact, it is very economical in terms of the continued survival of the species. After all, the main reason for the female's existence is to produce and ensure the survival of the offspring which carry her genes. The more food the young obtain, the faster they reach sexual maturity and again pass on those genes. It makes sense, then, for the female to assist their rapid development by providing a meal from her worn-out body rather than leaving it for some foraging scavenger to eat.

Despite the enormous disparity in the amount of time and effort devoted to parental care in the spiders, the populations of individual species tend to remain fairly constant. *Oonops*, for example, produces only two eggs at a time and takes no further interest in them, whereas *Dolomedes* lays up to 300, carries them around, wetting them at intervals, finally building the young a nursery, yet just two replacements are on average produced for each species from each pair of spiders.

Moulting

As the young spiders feed and grow they have to undergo a series of moults. Unlike the backboned animals, they are unable to grow gradually and, in common with other arthropods, they increase their size in a series of steps, shedding their hard exoskeleton at intervals and producing a new one. For a variable length of time prior to moulting, the spider ceases to feed and then hangs from some suitable structure by a short length of silk before becoming immobile. During this resting period, the new exoskeletal layers are forming beneath the old one and some of the material from the old exoskeleton is being reabsorbed back into the spider to minimise the amount of new building material that has to be called upon from its food reserves. As in the insects and crustaceans, the process of moulting, or *ecdysis* as it is scientifically called, is controlled by the hormone, *ecdysone*, and it commences when the old exoskeleton covering the carapace splits along the sides; movements of the spider then cause the split to pass backwards along the sides of the abdomen. The old exoskeleton gradually hinges away from the emerging spider and continued movements then result in the withdrawal of the appendages, just like fingers being removed from a pair of gloves. The moulting process is illustrated in Fig. 5.6 and Plate 5.8 shows a newly moulted spider in the act of stretching its new exoskeleton.

Moulting is assisted by the production of a fluid underneath the old skeleton, which separates it from the underlying layers which will produce the new exoskeleton. Once the fluid has fulfilled its function, it is reabsorbed and the gap which remains becomes filled with air, which makes for the easy separation of the old skeleton. Having escaped from the old exoskeleton, the spider, hanging still from the original silken thread, now expands its body to stretch the new skeleton to its full size, at the same time flexing all of its joints to keep them supple. The legs, in particular, are continually drawn in towards the body and then straightened out again and research has revealed that, if this movement is restricted, then the appendages become permanently distorted and incapable of being used normally. At first, the spider is very pale in colour, but, as the new exoskeleton dries and hardens, it gradually assumes its proper colouration. Once dry, the skeleton of the cephalothorax prevents any further growth in this region, but this is not true of the much softer abdomen with its more supple skeleton, which can accommodate the expansion involved as it becomes filled with eggs in the mature female.

The process of moulting is fraught with problems for the spiders and arthropods in general and many die as a result of it. In general, the process is faster and easier in young spiders and becomes progressively slower as the individual proceeds towards the final moult to the adult form. Apart from the dangers involved in the process itself, the spider is very vulnerable at this time and may itself become the prey of other creatures, which are normally the prey of the spider itself.

It is only after the final moult that the sex of the spider becomes apparent and it assumes the adult colouration, although sub-adult males of some species can be recognised by their rather swollen palps. The number of moults required from newly hatched spiderling to adult varies a great deal but appears to bear some relation to the final size of the adult spider, in that species with small adults tend to shed their exoskeleton fewer times than those which finally attain a large size. Thus the small money spiders moult only three times during their life, whereas a large female *Dolomedes* will have

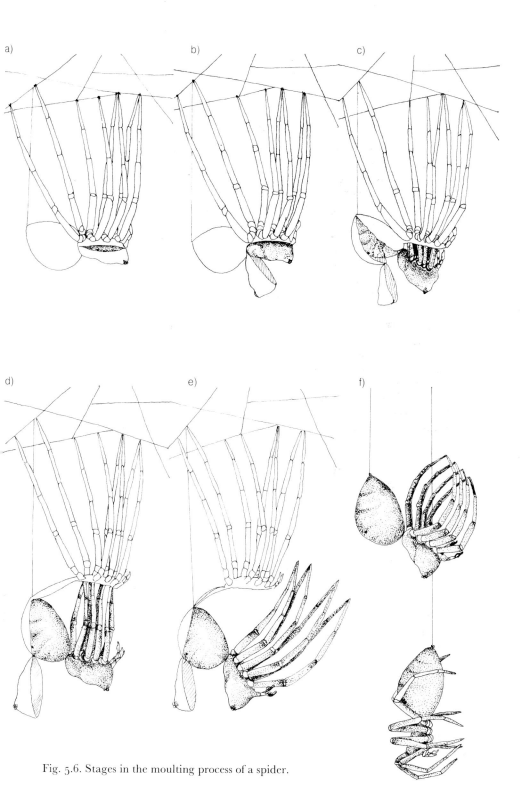

a)

b)

c)

d)

e)

f)

Fig. 5.6. Stages in the moulting process of a spider.

Plate 5.8. *Araneus quadratus*. A recently moulted female stretching her legs as the new exoskeleton dries and hardens. Europe.

undergone ten moults before reaching adulthood. Male spiders are often much smaller than their female counterparts and, in consequence, require fewer moults before they become adult, frequently reaching maturity before their prospective mates. This is a highly desirable arrangement in those species whose males court females who are in a helpless state immediately after moulting (Plate 1.2), mainly to reduce the likelihood of being eaten. In adult spiders, moulting appears to be limited to long-lived females of the more primitive types of spider, especially the mygalomorphs, presumably to replace structures essential to their survival which have become worn out during their long lives.

Regeneration

In common with many arthropods, spiders are able to regenerate lost appendages during their developmental stages, although the closer the spider is to maturity, the less likely it is that the lost appendage will assume its normal size and form. This is simply because a certain number of moults is required for full regeneration to occur. Once a spider is adult, this regenerative ability is lost, except in those long-lived mygalomorphs just mentioned, who can moult after reaching maturity.

Spiders also have the ability to lose a limb to escape when caught by a would-be predator, in much the same way that some lizards escape by shedding their tails. The limb breaks off at a weak point between the coxa and trochanter, where, by means of a special mechanism, the blood flow is quickly staunched or else the spider would soon die of haemorrhage. Since the spider has eight legs, it may be left at relatively little disadvantage with the loss of as many as four of them, as long as it retains at least one on one side and three on the other. This is not so for the crab spiders, which rely upon their large front legs for grasping prey, for if one or both of these is lost from one side then the spider is unlikely to be able to fend for itself. If a leg is merely torn off by a predator, rather than detached at the weak point, then the spider is in imminent danger of bleeding to death. Its instinctive reaction, therefore, is to bite off the remains of the leg at the weak point, which is then sealed off rapidly, and then to suck the juices from its own severed limb.

Dispersal

A very important part of the spider's life cycle is dispersal, since large numbers of them often hatch from individual egg-sacs leading to overcrowding. This soon leads to competition for limited food supplies which, in turn, can lead to a considerable amount of cannibalism. Spiders, of course, can disperse under their own power simply by walking away, but they also have their own unique method of dispersal by means of aeronautic behaviour, or *ballooning* as it is otherwise called. Many people have seen the results of such behaviour, probably without being aware of precisely what has taken place. It is common on warm summer and autumn days to find small spiders crawling around on one's clothes or hair, as if they had just dropped out of the sky. The likelihood is that this is exactly what they have done, using a length of silk still attached to their spinnerets as a parachute. The Linyphiid money spiders are by far the most common aeronauts in temperate regions of the northern hemisphere, although the pre-adults of many other spider families display such behaviour and, in a few cases, adults, especially males, may also disperse in this manner. In general, the more primitive spiders are not aeronauts, although, in Australia, young spiders of the mygalomorph, *Missulena*, have been observed using aerial dispersal, a possible explanation for the widespread occurrence of this genus of spiders throughout the whole of the Australian continent. A sub-adult wolf spider of the genus *Pardosa* is the largest aeronaut that the authors have seen but there are reports that the adult males of some orb web spiders disperse by ballooning.

The prerequisites for aerial dispersal appear to be that the spider must be light enough to be carried on a thin silken thread and that the meteorological conditions need to be just right. Aeronautic activity normally takes place on warm days rather than windy ones and recent research on one of the money spiders in Holland has shown that the wind speed must not exceed 11 kph (7 mph) at about 2 m (6½ ft) above the ground. Unstable air near the ground, such as results from air rising from warm earth, stimulates aerial activity.

A spider which is about to take off first climbs to the top of a grass stem, twig or post and stands facing into any light breeze which may be blowing at the time. It then stands on tiptoe and points its abdomen upwards (Fig. 5.7), at the same time releasing a stream of silk from the spinnerets. The silk rises upwards in the currents of warm air and, as soon as the pull on it is sufficient, the spider lets go and drifts up into the air.

The distances travelled by these intrepid aeronauts varies from a few metres to hundreds or even thousands of kilometres, since they are

Fig. 5.7. *Pardosa* sp. An immature wolf spider standing on tiptoe and pointing its abdomen upwards, at the same time releasing a silk thread, not visible here, before it takes off from the top of a wooden fence. Europe.

completely at the mercy of the prevailing air currents and spiders are often reported landing on ships far out at sea. Although they usually drift at fairly low levels, below 70 m (200 ft), spiders have been taken in aerial plankton samples at 3000 m (10 000 ft) and they may be quite common at 1500 m (5000 ft). Clearly many of them land in unsuitable places or are blown out to sea and drown, but sufficient of them must reach an acceptable environment for the ballooning phenomenon to have become so widespread amongst the spiders.

A special word, *gossamer*, has come into use to describe the masses of silk which may accumulate on vegetation, when many hundreds of thousands of spiders are dispersing from a particular area. The derivation of the word is probably from 'goose summer' because the gossamer resembles masses of goose down and usually appears in summer. As any one spider may have to produce several strands of silk before it can successfully take off, the spare strands often aggregate together to form what is referred to as gossamer, which may be even more noticeable when it glistens with dew in the early morning of a day following active dispersal on the previous day. In the past, masses of gossamer blowing in the air have been interpreted as objects from outer space or, on vegetation, as having come from alien spacecraft.

Longevity

Most spiders live for only one season, the males normally having shorter lives than the females, since once mated they are of no further use and die. In temperate regions, the females which have developed from eggs laid during the summer may overwinter and lay several batches of eggs during the following summer, thus surviving for at least a year. Some wolf and jumping spiders which hatch in the spring or early summer of one year may survive until the autumn of the following year, a life span of 18 months. Our domestic species, such as the house spider, *Tegenaria*, and the daddy-longlegs spider, *Pholcus*, may live considerably longer than this, perhaps cushioned from the extremes of climate by the relative cosiness of their human habitations.

The longest-lived spiders are almost certainly the females of the myg-alomorphs, already mentioned twice before with regard to their ability to moult and regenerate once they have attained maturity. These remarkable spiders have been reported as taking up to 12 years to mature and, therefore, their total lifespan must be considerably longer. An adult spider of this type was once kept for 5 years in a laboratory, having been collected as a mature individual of unknown age from the wild, so it would have been at least 17 years old at death, if not older.

Apart from dying of old age, a spider's life may be terminated in many different ways, some obvious, some less so. The more obvious ones include starvation, cannibalism, aeronauting into an unsuitable place or being exposed to extreme climatic conditions, as well as falling prey to predators such as birds, reptiles and insectivorous mammals. They do, however, have some more insidious enemies and, as a result of some excellent television documentaries, one group of these may already be familiar to a number of readers. These are the spider-hunting wasps (Plate 5.9), the most spectacular of which, the tarantula hawks, prey upon the large, burrowing American mygalomorphs, although countless other species from all around the world are specialised for taking spiders of all sizes. These wasps all have in common their ability to approach a spider, itself a ferocious predator, and disable it using their sting without the hapless victim being able to retaliate in any way. It would appear that, in the presence of the wasp, the spider is completely mesmerised and thus easily captured. The sting only paralyses the spider, which is then dragged away to the wasp's burrow. It is sometimes possible to find a comatose spider hanging from a low piece of vegetation (Plate 5.10) where it has been left while the wasp is getting its bearings or is digging or opening its burrow ready to receive it. In its drugged state in the burrow, the spider awaits its fate at the jaws of the larva which hatches from the egg laid by the wasp. Some details of the ways in which the spiders attempt to avoid the depredations of these wasps are given in Chapter 7.

Other types of parasitic wasp lay a single egg on a spider and the resultant larva slowly eats its host alive, increasing in size as the spider slowly shrinks to an empty husk (Plate 5.11). Certain species of Tachinid fly use similar techniques but, in this instance, the larva lives inside the spider as it feeds and grows. Earlier in the chapter (p. 86), the emergence of parasitic wasps from spider egg-sacs was discussed and, in fact, many species of such wasps specialise in parasitising spider eggs. One such wasp is well known to the

Plate 5.9. *Batozonellus fuliginosus*. A female hunting wasp dragging a paralysed spider back to her nest burrow dug into a sandy road in the Shimba Hills in Kenya.

Plate 5.10. *Batozonellus fuliginosus*. A female hunting wasp coming to collect a paralysed spider which she had temporarily lodged in a tuft of grass while she went to open her burrow. Kenya.

authors and is associated with the spider, *Segestria senoculata*, a species which can be very common in the crevices of old walls in Britain. In such a crevice, the spider constructs a silk-lined tube from the outer end of which radiates a number of silken strands which act as trip wires. The spider waits in the tube and, if an insect touches one of these trip wires, it darts out and grabs it. The way in which the wasp prevents itself from becoming a meal for the spider is

Plate 5.11. Larva of a parasitic wasp attached to the spider which it is slowly eating alive. Australia.

fascinating to watch. It walks around on the wall, antennae all aquiver and seems to be able to sense the presence of the spider's tube from some distance away, for it slows down and approaches very warily, carefully feeling ahead with its antennae. When these eventually come into contact with the trip wire of an occupied tube, out comes the spider but, somehow, the wasp manages to jump backwards out of range. This may be repeated two or three times until the wasp decides that this particular tube is not safe and continues on its way. Its patience is eventually rewarded when, on finding an unoccupied tube, it backs into and lays its eggs on the egg-sac contained therein. Not all of the insect enemies of spiders are wasps. In Central America, a particular species of damselfly has been seen to feed specifically on orb web spiders, which it plucks out of the centres of their webs and, from Australia, it has been reported that the large *Nephila* females are bitten on the abdomen by blood-sucking sandflies.

Spiders may also succumb to infection by parasitic worms of the family Mermithidae. These roundworms inhabit the abdomen of the host spider and, as they grow, they may actually break out through the abdominal wall, without initially killing the spider. Two British researchers recently reported finding such a worm in a specimen of the small wolf spider, *Pardosa hortensis*. The spider itself averages only 5 mm ($\frac{3}{16}$ in) in length, yet the worm taken from it was 93 mm (over $3\frac{1}{2}$ in) long with an average diameter of less than 0.5 mm (about $\frac{1}{64}$ in). Put into perspective, this would be equivalent to a human being parasitised by a worm 30 m (100 ft) and 10 cm (4 in) in diameter.

Finally, many spiders are killed by fungi very similar to the entomophagous fungi that kill insects, especially flies, in very large numbers. The fungal infection slowly spreads through the tissues of the spider, which becomes lethargic and eventually dies. The white reproductive structures of the fungus then erupt through the body wall of the spider to release spores which are blown through the air to infect other spiders.

Chapter 6
Prey Capture

In most people's minds, the word spider is almost synonymous with that most wonderful of its creations, the orb web, and yet this is but one of the multifaceted methods by which spiders secure for themselves a living from the multitude of other small creatures which share their habitat. Whether a spider spends all of its life in a burrow or is constantly on the move, like the jumping spiders, it has inevitably, in its own way, solved the problem of obtaining sufficient food to grow and to continue its species. Some of the methods employed are bizarre in the extreme, as will be seen when the ogre-faced spiders and the bolas spiders are described (pp. 132–5). Within the spiders, there are four main approaches to prey capture although, with each different approach, a considerable diversity of methods may be used. First there are the sedentary mygalomorphs, which include the trapdoor spiders, the sheet web tarantulas and the purse web spiders. Next are the spiders which play the waiting game, lying in ambush for their prey on bark or flowers; the crab spiders are typical examples of this. Following these are those agile, fast-moving spiders which run down their prey without the use of silk or a fixed home, spiders such as the wolf and jumping spiders. Finally, there are the web-building spiders, who have achieved the ultimate perfection in the use of silk to secure them a living.

Mygalomorphs

Trapdoor Spiders

Female trapdoor spiders are amongst the most sedentary of all spiders, often spending the whole of their considerable life spans entombed within the secure walls of their silken burrows, lying within the protective embrace of the earth itself. Trapdoor spiders are almost exclusively nocturnal and, as night falls, many species will gently raise the silken door at the entrance to their burrows, holding it ajar by putting forth their head and front two pairs of legs. Most of these spiders prefer moist situations where plenty of insects are likely to pass by. Those which trespass too close to the burrow entrance are seized by the spider in a lightning swoop of the front legs while its back legs are kept securely in the burrow, enabling a rapid retreat if danger threatens. Once subdued, the prey is dragged into the burrow and consumed at the spider's leisure. Occasionally, the spider will leave the safety of its burrow for a brief instant to pursue and overcome an insect which cannot be reached from within the burrow, but this is only done in extreme cases because the spider is a clumsy creature once outside the familiar surroundings of its silken tube. All kinds of running and crawling insects are taken, including ground beetles, ants and grasshoppers and, in areas of semi-desert, a cluster of trapdoors may be found in a favourable area around the base of a tree, where the spiders take a heavy toll of young locust hoppers. Any insects which are found to be unpalatable are unceremoniously ejected from the burrow a second or two after their capture.

There has been a considerable amount of argument about the way in which a spider, which is insulated from the sights and sounds of the outside world, within a subterranean burrow, is able to detect the presence of prey. Those species which protrude the front part of their body outside their trapdoor can obviously use the sensitive hairs and trichobothria on their legs to pick up the vibrations produced by a moving insect both in the air and through the ground. Sight may also play a part since, in Australia, it has been found that trapdoor spiders inhabiting leaf litter, where visibility is restricted by the clutter of leaves, had small eyes, whereas spiders inhabiting more open areas had larger eyes, which could be more fully employed looking for the movements of approaching insects across the more open spaces.

Some trapdoor species, however, do not open their doors in the evening but leap out unerringly upon a passing insect which has been detected from within the burrow. During studies of the American spider, *Ummidia carabivora*, which positions itself at nightfall beneath the fractionally open trapdoor with its legs in contact with the undersurface, it was found that sensitivity to vibrations of passing insects seemed to be distinctly lacking, for in over 95% of cases of prey capture, the insect actually had to walk over the top of the trapdoor before being detected. *Ummidia* lunged at the prey with the front half of its body, striking with amazing rapidity, the time taken from starting the lunge to contacting the prey averaging only 0.03 seconds. The spider's accuracy was high, with only a little over 10% of the strikes missing their target, which one must remember had not been visible until a split second before the spider struck. It seems, therefore, that in *Ummidia*, and possibly in many other trapdoor spiders, habitats are selected where insects are in sufficient numbers to ensure a reasonable chance of having one regularly stumble across a trapdoor, the efficiency of the prey capture then ensuring that, even if it happens only occasionally, a chance to take a meal is seldom missed.

Those mygalomorph spiders which habitually rush out of their burrows to catch a passing insect, normally construct their doors of wafer-thin silk and they stay open while the spider is absent and do not hinder a rapid re-entry.

These spiders also have longer legs than their more sedentary kin and somewhat better eyesight. Other mygalomorphs have increased their chances of detecting passing prey by extending the range of their senses, rather in the way the orb web weavers use their webs to extend their tactile range. A number of species construct silken tripwires which radiate outwards from the burrow entrance so that small animals stumbling over them are instantly seized by the spider as it rushes out. In Australia, there are a number of mygalomorphs which go one step further by collecting twigs and arranging them in a radial pattern around the burrow entrance. *Arganippe raphiduca*, for example, lies in readiness just beneath her door, which is left slightly ajar, and uses the tips of her outstretched legs to maintain contact with the ends of the twigs. Any small animal running across the twig lines immediately conveys its presence, via the twigs, to the waiting spider.

'Tarantulas'

Included under this heading are the formidable members of the family Theraphosidae, known in the USA as tarantulas, although strictly speaking this name should be applied only to members of the true spider genus, *Lycosa*. In the tropics, there are a number of tree-dwelling species, such as *Avicularia*, which occasionally prey on birds, most probably hens incubating eggs, and they are consequently referred to as the bird-eating spiders. In the jungles of Brazil, the giant species of *Lasiodora* and *Grammostola* probably feed extensively on vertebrate animals, such as small snakes, lizards and frogs and, in captivity, they certainly prefer these small, cold-blooded animals to insects, when given the choice. Even small poisonous snakes may be killed, the spider catching hold of them by the head and hanging on until its poison starts to work and the snake becomes still. The spider then uses its powerful chelicerae to crush the snake into a shapeless pulp, starting at the head and gradually sucking the whole body dry. The whole process may take as long as a day.

Purse Web Spiders

The European purse web spider, *Atypus affinis* (Plate 6.1), is the only member

Plate 6.1. *Atypus affinis*. This is the only British mygalomorph spider, illustrated here by a female which has been carefully extricated from her purse web to be photographed.

of the mygalomorphs to extend into the British Isles and is a close relative of the trapdoor spiders. *Atypus* spends the whole of its life sealed within a silken tube, usually 200 to 230 mm (8 to 9 in) long and lacking any signs of an entrance or exit. The tubes are usually built into a sloping burrow dug into a bank with a small length of the tube left projecting above the ground like the finger of a glove. The projecting portion of the tube is usually covered with detritus from around the burrow, rendering it fairly invisible to the casual observer. Catching prey from within this sealed tube would seem to be somewhat of a problem for the spider and, for many years, it was thought that *Atypus* sallied forth after dark in search of food or else subsisted entirely on earthworms which accidentally crawled into her burrow. In reality, on detecting an insect or other arthropod prey, such as a centipede walking on the exposed portion of the tube, the spider spears it through the tube's silken wall, using her sharp, curved chelicerae. The spider then uses the teeth situated on the basal segment of the chelicerae to saw a hole through the silken tube and the prey is then dragged through this and into the burrow to be consumed (Fig. 6.1). Stowing her meal at the bottom of the burrow, the

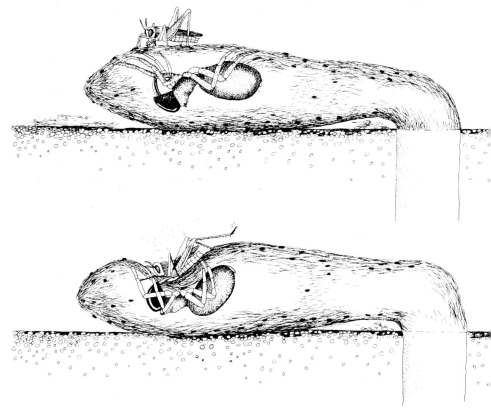

Fig. 6.1. A purse web spider, *Atypus*, catching a grasshopper by transfixing it with her fangs through the silken wall of her tube.

spider then returns to the cut in the tube and uses her jaws to hold the two edges of the cut together while repairing it with silk from her spinnerets. This way of life is typical of many other purse web spiders, the main variations between species being in the length of tube left protruding and its position. In some American species, for example, the tubes run from the mouth of the burrow and up adjacent trees for a short distance.

In the western USA, the turret spider, *Atypoides riversi*, makes long inclined burrows topped with a few centimetres of silken turret furnished with a collapsible collar for closing the open end. The outside of the collar is decorated with local materials such as moss, bits of lichen or pine needles. After dark, the spider perches in the entrance at the top of the turret, which provides an excellent watch-tower for spotting approaching insects.

True Spiders

Ambushing Spiders

Included here are the crab spiders and some of the less active of the lynx spiders, the latter normally being active hunters. The crab spiders are mainly slow-moving, squat-bodied spiders which bear a striking re-semblance to crabs, both in their shape and in their habit of always scuttling sideways or crabwise. The females are sedentary creatures, seldom moving far from a favourite perch in a flower or on a leaf, where they lie in ambush awaiting the arrival of some unsuspecting insect. A number of species may also be found on the bark of trees or on the ground or under stones, but it is those that live on flowers which tend most often to be noticed by the casual observer. While lying in wait on a flower, the two pairs of long front legs, strongly armed with bristles on their inner edges, are held out in anticipation, ready to fold inwards in a pincer movement on any insect which approaches too closely (Plate 6.2). The two rear pairs of legs hold firmly onto the flower, anchoring the spider against the brief struggles of a captured insect. As a victim alights on the flower, the crab spider may stealthily alter its position prior to the deadly embrace, detecting the prey by the vibrations and its reasonably acute forward vision. It is then that the front legs enfold the insect and the spider's fangs are embedded into the back of its neck. If, by miscalculation or the lack of a suitable opportunity, the spider initially bites the abdomen it will quickly transfer to the back of the neck. This particular bite is favoured because the insect's nerve cord passes through the neck and the spider's powerful nerve poison is quickly able to induce paralysis in the victim, thus reducing the time that it struggles in the spider's grip. As well as minimising the chances of the insect breaking free and escaping, rapid action of the poison is desirable because it minimises the risk of drawing the attention of a larger predator to the struggling duo. Crab spiders lack cheliceral teeth and so do not chew their food like many other spiders. As a result of this, and the position in which it is held by the spider,

Plate 6.2. A Kenyan crab spider feeds on a warningly coloured moth. Spiders are unable to appreciate these colours, which are intended to be seen by vertebrate predators, and this spider may eventually reject the moth if it is too unpleasant.

the apparently undamaged insect seemingly continues to feed on the flower in a natural-looking way, which scarcely betrays the position of the camouflaged spider.

A somewhat unusual crab spider, the long, slim, straw-coloured European species, *Tibellus oblongus*, usually sits head downward along a grass stem and flings itself upon passing insects. It will occasionally take other spiders as prey when the chance is offered. The crab spiders will often take amazingly large insects and the white, or sometimes yellow, *Misumena vatia* (Plate 6.3) seems adept at subduing stinging insects, such as hive bees, and even large and formidable bumblebees. Quite large butterflies, including, in Britain, the marbled white and the meadow brown, are frequently caught by *Misumena*, their wings sometimes held out in a heraldic pose as the spider quietly sucks them dry. Even the smaller *Xysticus* species, half the size of *Misumena*, can manage a fairly large butterfly, although they tend to concentrate mainly upon flies, especially hoverflies. Many of these hoverflies have a black and yellow striped abdomen, mimicking the patterns of wasps, thereby normally giving them a degree of protection against potential predators. That this mimicry of a distasteful or dangerous insect is aimed at vertebrate predators such as birds is made clear from the way in which these

Plate 6.3. *Misumena vatia*. The less common yellow form of this crab spider sits in her normal pose as she waits for prey to alight on the flower. Europe and USA.

wasp-mimicking hoverflies are instantly attacked and killed by crab spiders. The latter will indeed retreat from a genuine wasp, thereby indicating that the spider is reacting to some stimulus other than the striped warning colours of the wasp. Occasionally crab spiders may be seen taking a short cut to a meal and *Xysticus cristatus*, for example, has been seen by the authors stealthily feeding on a fly caught in the web of a garden spider, while the rightful owner of the meal was feeding from the opposite side, totally unaware of the crab spider's intrusion.

Hunting Spiders

In this category may be included a range of spiders from many different families but all having in common the fact that, in one way or another, they actively go in search of their prey rather than waiting for it to come to them. At one extreme are the short-sighted hunters, which often spend the hours of daylight under stones or pieces of bark or wood, emerging at night to pounce upon insects located by their questing front legs. At the other extreme are the agile, long-sighted hunters, who scamper around on vegetation during the day, either running down or pouncing upon prey picked out by their highly effective eyes.

One of the nocturnal hunters is *Dysdera crocata*, a rather fierce-looking but handsome spider with a brick red carapace and legs and a pale grey or white abdomen, which may now be found under stones in many parts of the world, since it is one of those species which has been spread accidentally by man.

Occupying much of the spider's front end are the jutting chelicerae, each of which carries an enormous fang, for which the spider has a special use. Sharing *Dysdera*'s damp habitat are numbers of woodlice, slow-moving crustaceans which have become adapted to live on land, assisted by their armoured exoskeleton and their nasty-tasting body fluids. The fangs of most spiders are unable to penetrate the body armour of the woodlouse, which in any case would be rejected on account of its taste. Not so *Dysdera*, which is a specialist, her clumsy, slow-moving gait and short sight being no encumbrance in her pursuit of the equally slow-moving woodlice. Encountering one of these on her nocturnal ramblings, *Dysdera* responds by twisting her cephalothorax to enable one fang to pierce the soft underparts while the other fang penetrates the dorsal armour. Not every species of woodlouse is taken as some are too distasteful even for *Dysdera*'s specialised tastes.

There are many other spiders which like *Dysdera* are nocturnal hunters and are therefore seldom seen by the majority of people. Much more often seen, in fact often hard to miss, are the wolf spiders, day-active hunters with a good turn of speed and excellent eyesight but, unlike their mammalian namesakes, solitary rather than hunting in packs. Although mainly ground-dwelling in habit, they do venture onto vegetation and a few live on the trunks of trees, which incidentally happens to be the main hunting ground of the giant crab spiders of the family Sparassidae and the two-tailed spiders, the Hersiliidae. Perhaps the most familiar of the wolf spiders are members of the genus *Pardosa*, which occupy an enormous range of habitat: the seashore, fields and gardens, riverbanks, sand dunes, woodlands and even the exposed jumble of stones and boulders on high northern mountains. Superficially, they look very similar, with drab browns and blacks dominating their colouration but, in fact, a large number of different species of *Pardosa* are found around the world. Closely related are the *Pirata* species, their name indicating an association with water, across the surface of which they are able to skim with consummate ease. The genus *Lycosa*, which includes the true tarantula from Europe, consists of generally larger and more handsomely marked species than *Pirata* and some American ones are distinctively striped. A proportion of *Lycosa* species are not, however, truly nomadic, having evolved the ability to dig burrows, in which they spend a large part of their lives.

Whatever their life styles, the wolf spiders are heavily dependent on their eyesight. The head is typically squared off at the sides with two large eyes and four smaller eyes facing forwards, giving excellent frontal vision, while two small eyes high up on top of the head extend the range of vision to the sides and to a certain extent to the rear. With this battery of acutely perceptive eyes, the spider can detect moving prey at a distance of several centimetres. Upon spotting a victim, the wolf spider creeps stealthily towards it, finally putting on a burst of speed before leaping onto the prey, which it then pierces with it fangs in the usual spider manner. Insects which remain motionless are in less danger than those which betray their presence

Fig. 6.2. *Pisaura mirabilis*. A male nursery web spider consuming a Bibionid fly. Europe.

by moving, for such movements are important in triggering pursuit in wolf spiders.

Pisaura mirabilis from Europe and the similar *Pisaurina* species from the USA are rather like slimmer, longer-legged versions of *Pardosa* and hunt their prey in a similar way upon vegetation (Fig. 6.2), but the most formidable hunters of the family Pisauridae are the various *Dolomedes* species. The British *Dolomedes fimbriatus* is a widely distributed, large, chocolate-and-cream-coloured spider, which preys mainly upon insects which have fallen into pools upon the surface of which the spider skilfully hunts. All *Dolomedes* live in marshy and swampy areas, usually spending their day sitting upon a floating leaf of some aquatic plant. On closer examination, it will be seen that the spider keeps its front legs in contact with the surface of the water, where they are in a position to detect vibrations set up by a small fish swimming or an insect struggling at the water surface. The bulk of the food of these spiders undoubtedly consists of terrestrial insects from the vegetation around the pool, which have accidentally fallen into the water, as well as aquatic insects or insects which have come to lay their eggs in the pool. Diving below the surface to catch prey is not a normal method for *Dolomedes* spiders, which being large, have to make a considerable effort to break the water's surface film and can submerge only by thrusting against some anchored support with their back legs. They have, however, been observed catching small fish and tadpoles, hence their American name of fisher spiders. The spider's strong jaws and potent venom rapidly overcome even vertebrate prey, which is effectively digested by the spider's digestive juices. Sometimes there may be a considerable struggle on the surface of the water if a large and vigorous victim is being attacked, but the victorious spider eventually carries her prey back onto a floating leaf or on to land to commence her meal. Some fisher spiders actually attract prey within reach by sitting on a floating leaf in the normal way but with their legs dabbling gently in the water. Like the wriggling of the angler's worm, these movements attract small fishes within range where the spider can pounce on them, using the excellent eyesight it has in common with the wolf spiders.

Perhaps strangest of all spider hunting methods is that employed by the European water spider, *Argyroneta aquatica*, an inhabitant of still ponds and lakes. *Argyroneta* is able to spend its life below water by constructing a diving bell in which she can breathe air, while waiting for prey to swim past. The construction of the bell is an amazing accomplishment for a spider and well worth examining in more detail, as it is vital to the whole life of the spider. First she weaves a small silken platform, which is anchored to submerged water plants. Then she swims or crawls to the surface and, in a complex movement involving her hind legs and the rear of the abdomen, she traps a bubble of air. Climbing back down below the silk platform head first, she releases the bubble from between her back legs and it floats up to be trapped below the silk, which now becomes the roof of the bell. More air is released from the tip of the abdomen and she will sometimes stroke off tiny bubbles using her hind tarsi. With her first load of air safely trapped beneath the silk, she normally spends some time extending and strengthening the bell before going back to the surface for further supplies of air. She works hard at building her home, making up to six trips to the surface before the bell, which does resemble a bell-jar in appearance, contains sufficient air for her to remain in it (Fig. 6.3).

Once her home is complete, *Argyroneta* is ready to commence hunting. She sits, snug in her bell, with her long legs sticking out below, ready to sense the approach of suitable prey. Her sensitivity to vibrations in the water is so finely developed that she can even detect an insect struggling on the surface of the water above her. On detecting a suitable water organism within range, she leaves the bell and pounces upon it, grasping it with her legs and pulling it towards her gaping fangs, ever prepared to deliver their deadly bite. She then tows the prey back to the bell and commences feeding. Both *Argyroneta* and *Dolomedes* must feed out of water, which would otherwise dilute the enzymes poured on to the prey to such an extent that digestion just would not take place.

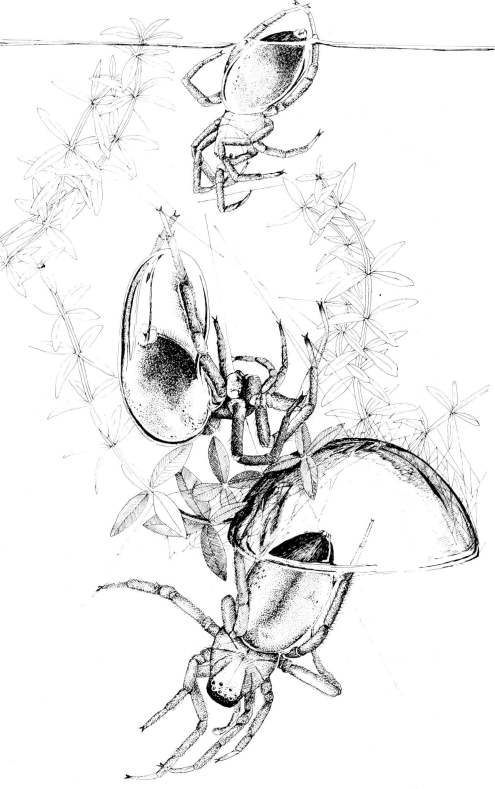

Fig. 6.3. The water spider, *Argyroneta aquatica*. In this sequence, a female collects a bubble of air from the surface and carries it down to release it into her partly built underwater home. When complete this resembles a thimble. Europe.

Jumping and Lynx Spiders

The jumping spiders are usually considered to have reached the peak of achievement in active hunting of prey by spiders, although the somewhat larger but normally less conspicuous lynx spiders are just as agile and efficient. The jumping spiders, however, are more cosmopolitan and therefore will receive more attention here than the mainly tropically and sub-tropically distributed lynx spiders.

The majority of jumping spiders are sun-lovers and they are perfectly adapted for their lives as wandering, sharp-eyed hunters. Their most immediately obvious asset is their large front eyes, which attract instant attention from the observer by their habit of peering closely at him in a manner not normally expected from such a tiny invertebrate, more like a curious cat than a spider. They are often rather confiding little creatures, showing little sign of fear of so large an animal as a human being and the common zebra spider, *Salticus scenicus*, so frequently found on the walls and windows of human habitations during the summer, can easily be persuaded to jump onto an outstretched finger, where it will sit eyeing you with obvious interest. In reality, of course, it is considering whether or not the movements associated with this large object mean that a meal is at hand. One cannot help getting the impression, however, that their perception of the world around them is very different from that of all other spiders and this gives them an aura of personality which sets them apart from their spider brethren.

There are no large jumping spiders, most being less than 15 mm ($\frac{5}{8}$ in) in length. They are most common in the tropics where many species are brilliantly marked (Plates 3.7 & 8) which more than makes up for their

Fig. 6.4. A jumping spider (family Salticidae). Trinidad.

Fig. 6.5. *Hyllus* sp. A jumping spider with its homopteran prey. Borneo.

diminutive stature. The visual ability of these spiders has already been discussed in Chapter 2, but it is worth re-affirming that they are able to spot movements of possible prey from a considerable distance, which accounts for the way in which they react to an approaching human being, and they are able to form clear images from several centimetres using their large front eyes. For spiders which display such ability as jumpers, their legs are surprisingly short and sturdy, with no obvious modifications to send them leaping around with such prowess. They can perform amazing leaps up to forty times their own body length and this ability can probably be explained by their small size and their very light weight. It is worth remembering that even smaller leapers, such as fleas, are able to jump even greater distances in relation to their body length.

Jumping spiders are often found running around on leaves, the trunks of trees, rocks or walls, moving their heads from side to side as they search for their prey. Once located, the prey is stalked much as a cat stalks a mouse before the final pounce, which nine times out of ten is bang on target. Some species live on vertical surfaces and can even run on the surface of glass, aided by the scopulae on their feet. Like all of their kin they never lose contact with the silken life-line which is constantly trailed behind them as they hunt and is

Plate 6.4. A pretty jumping spider feeding on a butterfly in a rain forest in Peru.

securely fastened down at intervals, especially before a jump is attempted. In this manner, they are brought up short if they fall as they nimbly jump from plant to plant or if a capture leap is badly misjudged. On occasion, they have even been seen to leap away from a vertical surface to seize insects in flight, a remarkable example of co-ordination between their sensory and locomotory systems.

A variety of prey is taken by jumping spiders, although it is not always actively hunted down, some species preferring to spend most or part of the time waiting for prey to come to them. Other spiders sometimes form part of their diet but flies, bugs and small beetles are the most common prey, although they can tackle such things as damselflies and remarkably large butterflies and moths (Plate 6.4). Even large and vigorous insects, such as grasshoppers and the smaller bush crickets (katydids), are taken, presumably being incapacitated by the spider's rapid-acting poison before they can use their own jumping powers to pull themselves free of the spider's grasp. In South-East Asia, some jumping spiders have adopted the unusual habit of preying upon orb web spiders, leaping onto them as they sit in their webs and consuming them on the spot.

The lynx spiders tend to be somewhat slimmer and longer-legged than the jumping spiders, but like them they run around actively on vegetation, jumping from leaf to leaf in search of their prey. They are also sun-lovers, with good eyesight and a jumping ability that almost matches that of the jumping spiders. Many of them are green in colour and this successfully

Plate 6.5. *Peucetia* sp. A lynx spider with dragonfly prey in a Kenyan forest habitat.

camouflages those more sedentary species which sit on leaves and wait for their prey to come to them (Plate 6.5).

Pirate Spiders

Perhaps some of the strangest of all spiders are the members of the family Mimetidae, the pirate spiders. The name pirate spiders is something of a misnomer, for pirates are normally associated with looting and pillaging, whereas the Mimetidae are not interested in the prey of other spiders but in the spiders themselves. There are three pirate spiders in the British Isles, all belonging to the genus *Ero*, which are small with a hunched-back look about them and with prettily marked abdomens. These slow-moving spiders lack the agility and sharp sight necessary to hunt insect prey, yet neither do they spin a web of their own to serve the same purpose. Instead, they have adopted the life of the stealthy intruder, invading the webs of other spiders and killing and feeding on the occupants.

Ero seems to prey mainly on Theridiids, many of which have a powerful poison of their own, capable of killing insects as big as bumblebees, so she must act with considerable circumspection to avoid being detected by her victim before she herself is ready to pounce. Entering the web of a *Theridion*,

Ero creeps carefully along a thread, moving with such caution that the occupant cannot detect her intrusion onto the web. She then stops and bites away some of the web to clear a space in front of her before gently tugging at a line to attract the attention of the *Theridion*. The latter, believing the intruder to be an insect, swoops down, only to be seized in a surprise attack by *Ero*, who pierces the femur of a front leg with her chelicerae. Instead of the grim struggle which one might expect to ensue, nothing of the sort happens, the *Theridion* just drops dead, killed almost instantaneously by the potent poison injected by *Ero*'s fangs. That she should have evolved such a potent venom is not all surprising in view of her need to invade the webs of spiders, who themselves are efficient killers, and to subdue them before they can retaliate in any way. It is interesting to note that, if the victim happens to get bitten in the abdomen rather than the leg, the poison acts more slowly, taking up to 30 seconds to do its work.

Web-Building Spiders

A large number of spiders belonging to various families employ silk in one way or another to assist in the capture of prey. The best known examples are the symmetrical orb webs of the Araneidae, such as *Araneus* and *Argiope*, which act as aerial traps for flying insects (Fig. 6.6). Many other spiders

Fig. 6.6. *Araneus diadematus*. A female European garden spider in her web with her silk-swathed grasshopper prey.

build equally complex but less visually attractive structures, such as sheet and hammock webs, more suited to trap insects which walk or hop rather than fly, while a few, such as the spitting and bolas spiders, have evolved highly specialised methods of prey capture. As similar kinds of webs may be constructed by unrelated spiders, they will be considered under the type of web they produce rather than in family groupings, with examples of more typical types of web and some unusual examples as well.

HAMMOCK AND SHEET WEB SPIDERS Large sheet webs are constructed by a number of mygalomorphs, especially in the tropics, but to the observer in temperate countries, the pre-eminent webs in this group are made by the numerous tiny money spiders of the family Linyphiidae and by the drab, brown Agelenidae. In terms of sheer numbers, the hammock webs of the Linyphiids dominate the scene for in a typical area of rough grassland, there may be several score to the square metre and fifty or more webs may be crowded onto a large gorse bush. With the majority of these webs spanning just a few centimetres, their abundance is seldom recognised until a dewy autumn morning reveals them in all their shimmering splendour, carpeting a meadow with silver where the day before only the dull green of grass was visible. Linyphiids are the dominant spiders over the whole of the north temperate region, exceeding by a large margin the total number of all other kinds of spider, so the success of the hammock web in trapping insect prey must be considerable.

Just about every garden in Britain must have a resident population of *Linyphia triangularis*, one of the larger and more conspicuous of the family, whose hammock web (Plate 6.6) can attain 300 mm (12 in) in diameter. A typical British hedgerow may contain thousands of these webs, which consist of an intricate but rather haphazard mass of threads, which arise from the upper surface of the hammock to form a scaffold. In some species, notably the common American species, *L. marginata*, (also found in Europe but rare in Britain), the scaffold pulls the hammock upwards into a distinct dome but, in the majority of species, the hammock is flat or sags very slightly like a real hammock. The web of *L. triangularis* is slightly domed and lacks any form of retreat, the spider hanging upside down on the underside of the hammock, poised to pounce upon any insect which chances to fall upon the upper surface. None of the threads is sticky, an unnecessary complication for trapping the rather clumsy insects, such as froghoppers, which constitute the typical prey and which are tripped by the tangle of scaffolding threads and fall helplessly onto the hammock below. Once there, the insect blunders around as if intoxicated, being constantly tripped by the maze of threads which radiate upwards from the hammock surface. Few insects manage to get far before being overtaken by the *Linyphia*, who can move at ease across the web's surface. Spearing the insects from below with her fangs, she pulls her victim down through the hammock and away from the damaged area to wrap it in a silken shroud. Later on, the hole in the web will be repaired by

Plate 6.6. *Linyphia triangularis*. A dew-covered web of this very common Linyphiid on an English hedgerow.

laying a new sheet of silk across the torn surface.

Among the Agelenidae, the large sheet webs of the European *Agelena* and the American *Agelenopsis* species operate in a similar way and are equally effective in trapping hopping insect prey. A silken funnel leads away from the centre of the large *Agelena* webs (Plate 4.7) and the female sits on the entrance with her feet touching the sheet, ready to respond to any intruding insect. She is extremely sensitive to any movements of the web due to an insect blundering around on it and she responds to such a stimulus by darting nimbly across the sheet and sinking her fangs a number of times into her victim until it weakens and dies. It is then carried back to the safety of the funnel to be consumed.

Familiar to many people are the sheet webs of the large, hairy spiders of the genus *Tegenaria*. These include the house spiders whose webs cause so much panic among some housewives, for they are frequently constructed in the corners of box-rooms, garages and sheds and elsewhere in and around human habitations. Other *Tegenaria* species occur outside, building their webs in the angles of walls, between rocks and in the hollows of trees in shady woodland. They would appear to be rather less efficient than those of *Agelena*, since they lack the tangled mass of scaffolding which serves so well to bring down flying or hopping insects onto the main sheet of the web.

SCAFFOLD WEB SPIDERS Spiders which construct this type of web are restricted to the Theridiidae, and the small family Nesticidae, many of whose members are cave-dwellers and will not be considered here. The Theridiids are small globular spiders, which in some habitats may be found in large numbers, and they number among their company the famous black widow spider. Their webs can best be described as an intersecting mass of scaffold

Fig. 6.7. A Theridiid scaffold web. An insect blundering into the sticky base of the vertical lines easily detaches it from the ground. The elastic line then contracts, lifting the insect off the ground, and the spider then hauls it up into the web.

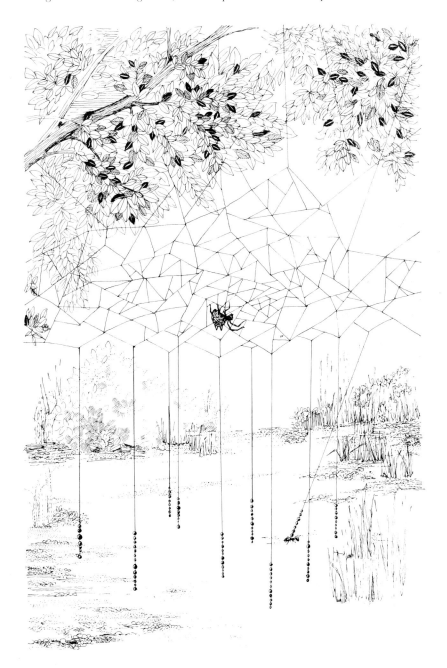

work with a central area consisting of a three-dimensional trellis of silk (Fig. 6.7). The actual arrangement of the lines varies between species, but the design is not as haphazard as it first appears and there is an underlying precision in the construction which only becomes evident upon closer examination. Droplets of glue adorn some of the threads, their placing depending on whether the web is for catching crawling or flying insects.

One of the commonest European members of the family is *Theridion sisyphium*, whose maternal devotion to her offspring has already been described in Chapter 5. The untidy-looking webs of this species are slung above the ground on tall herbs, bushes and small trees. They are designed to catch flying insects and so threads bearing the sticky droplets are incorporated in the central trellis work. The numerous hollow corpses of small flying insects, which are usually found incorporated in the silk around the spider's retreat, bear mute testimony to the efficiency of this web arrangement.

A number of other Theridiids have adapted their web to capture crawling insects, including the ants which are rejected by so many other predators, and by most spiders. *Achaearanea riparia*, a widely distributed European species rare in Britain, constructs an expansive, irregular scaffold web which is suspended beneath any overhanging plants and contains a large tent-like structure in the centre. The snare is anchored to the ground by means of a number of vertical threads which are coated with sticky globules on their lower ends. A crawling insect has to negotiate this barrage of sticky lines (Fig. 6.7) and easily becomes ensnared. Its struggles easily tear the lines free of the ground and the tightly stretched silk, which is very elastic, then contracts, pulling the insect with it. The spider then hauls it up into the web but, instead of biting it, she first covers it in sticky threads from her spinnerets to subdue it. The prey is then bitten, mainly on the legs, and the typically virulent Theridiid poison soon extinguishes the last signs of the victim's life.

Although of small size and somewhat portly build, Theridiids will tackle large and violent prey such as wasps, which powerful spiders such as the garden spider will hurriedly cut free from their webs, keeping their distance as they do so. The common *Enoplognatha ovata* seems to be afraid of nothing and will bustle down to do battle with any insect, regardless of size or its ability to sting. She is aided by her habit of flinging sticky threads over the insect, while keeping at a safe distance, reducing the capabilities of her victim to retaliate and allowing her in for a quick bite without being harmed. After several such lightning attacks, the prey's struggles become weaker as the poison begins to take effect and the spider can then go closer to wrap a thicker blanket of silk around it. Large wasps, bumblebees (Fig. 6.8) and hive bees are all overcome, despite their stinging ability which would almost certainly mean instant death to the spider, while large flies fall an easy victim. Despite their hard exoskeletons, beetles and weevils also feature prominently in the detritus of Theridiid webs, the spider's tiny fangs obviously being able to locate chinks in their armour.

Fig. 6.8. *Enoplognatha ovata*. This Theridiid spider has caught a bumblebee much bigger and more powerful than herself, which she has rapidly subdued with her potent venom. Europe and USA.

The intrinsic strength of this type of web is remarkable and, in the USA, the large snare of *Achaearenea tepidariorum* has been known to subdue a small mouse, which, despite its struggles, was lifted completely off the floor and killed. In contrast, the European species of *Episinus* have reduced the web almost to its logical limit, merely retaining two vertical strands of silk which are held apart by the spider's legs as she hangs downwards between them. The lower ends of these two threads are attached to the ground and are covered in sticky droplets, which trap passing insects.

ORB WEB SPIDERS The orb web with its elegant spirals is undoubtedly the most familiar of objects created by spiders, although it may only be noticed on autumn mornings when a heavy dew emphasises its radial perfection with baubles of shining liquid or when, in early winter, it is coated with a rime of hoar frost (Plate 6.7). At other times they may well be missed, unless the plump occupant can be seen sitting head downwards in the centre of its almost invisible web. In the design and manufacture of the orb web, spiders have attained the pinnacle of achievement in the use of silk and their dependence upon the web to secure a food supply is reflected in the large amount of space in the abdomen occupied by silk glands in these spiders. The majority of orb webs are the products of spiders belonging to the Araneidae,

Plate 6.7. *Araneus diadematus*. The orb web of the garden spider outlined in hoar frost. Europe.

although members of the cribellate family, Uloboridae, have independently achieved the same results, as will be shown later.

The orb webs of Araneids are slung in a variety of places; they may for instance be extremely numerous along hedges bordered on either side by arable fields or in virgin forests far from civilisation, high amongst the leaves of some ancient oak. As a trap for flying insects, the orb web is supremely efficient, sieving the air continuously as long as it remains undamaged and communicating its success in capturing some unfortunate insect to the waiting spider through the vibrations set up in it spokes. It has the advantage that it works 24 hours per day, exploiting both day- and night-flying insects, which are denied to builders of other types of web except by chance. Its silk is immensely strong and elastic and yet almost invisible, so that it behaves as a flexible net whose sticky lines effectively neutralise the struggles of all but the most powerful of flying insects.

On observing the delicate symmetrical perfection of the orb web, it is scarcely credible that it has been manufactured by the spider that is often to be seen sitting at its centre. The greatest puzzle is how on earth she ever manages to make a start on so complex a creation, especially the upper line which supports the web, as this may have to span a metre or more between two trees or bushes. In some of the tropical *Nephila*, this first line may cross small rivers and may be several metres in length. Whichever species of spider is considered and whatever the individual variations in the web, i.e. whether it is horizontally or vertically aligned, complete or with spirals missing, or ornamented with zig-zag lines of silk (the stabilimentum), there is always a set order of doing things to which the spider slavishly adheres. It is important to realise that the creation of this intricate design is not the act of an intelligent, reasoning creature but is an instinctive act, following a set of instructions inherited by each generation of spiders from its parents. Thus the ability to construct an orb web is already within the spiderlings when they hatch from the egg-sac and they can produce amazingly symmetrical webs a relatively short time after hatching. There is, however, a certain amount of flexibility inherent within the instinctive behavioural patterns which allows the spider to modify some details of the web to accommodate variations in the size and shape of the space available for its construction and also variations in weather conditions.

The European garden spider, *Araneus diadematus*, can be used as a typical example to illustrate the methods involved in orb web construction, methods which hold good for the majority of orb web spiders worldwide. An outline of the steps involved is shown in Fig. 6.9. The first line to be laid down must be the topmost bridging line, for it is from this that the whole web will be suspended, and this may be achieved in two ways. In the first place, a silk thread from the spinnerets can be drifted across the space in which the web is to be built, using air currents. When this drifting line catches on some object on the far side of the space, the spider hauls it in until it is tight and then anchors it at her end. She then crawls across this initial line of thin silk, spinning behind her a second, much thicker and stronger line to form the bridge-line proper. She may eat the original line, to conserve protein, or she may leave it to reinforce the bridge-line. The second way of setting up the bridge-line is for the spider to make her way across the space by climbing across vegetation, arching over the space to be used for the web, making sure that, all the time, the line is prevented from becoming entangled with any obstructions. The bridge-line is the most vital part of the whole web and once

Fig. 6.9. Stages in the construction of a typical orb web.

set up may be used over and over again to suspend new webs, so once it is established it is further reinforced with silk as the spider passes back and forth.

The spider now constructs the frame by first attaching a line to one side of the bridge-line and then trailing it across to the other side, where it is fixed, leaving a drooping silken thread hanging below the bridge-line. Returning to the bottom of this hanging loop of line, the spider then attaches a line to it and drops down until she reaches some object, whereupon she pulls on the silk until it is taut and then anchors it. She has now made a Y-shaped frame, known as the *first fork*, whose lines will form the web's primary radii and whose centre will form the hub of the web. Using the same technique as she used on the first fork, she now spins further sets of radial and frame threads, laying them across the triangles of the first fork. Using this frame as a base, the spider now adds the tertiary radii, starting from the centre and moving out to the frame to form each one. The radii are not laid down in a regular order but are simply added one at a time as she detects a gap with her legs while sitting in the centre of the web. By the time she has laid down the last radius, the web resembles the spokes of a wheel, the total number of radii varying with each species but seldom exceeding fifty. Now she moves to the centre of the web and turns round and round, spinning the spirals which form the hub. This done she now produces a set of temporary spirals, starting a little further out than the set she has just laid down at the centre of the web. The spider works outwards in a continuous spiral until the gap between the radii tells her that it is time to stop, at a distance somewhat short of the frame threads. Up to this point in the construction, she has used only dry silk but she now moves outwards beyond the scaffolding spirals and begins to lay down a sticky thread, circling inwards towards the centre of the web, removing and eating the scaffolding spirals as she proceeds, for they are no longer needed. The sticky silk is fastened to a radius, pulled towards the next, stretched with a snap, using the back legs and then fixed. This snapping action breaks the sticky coat on the thread into a series of beads like a miniature necklace. She performs this skilful task at speed, circling rapidly towards the hub but stopping short before she reaches the centre spirals, leaving a gap called the *free zone* between the sticky and dry spirals. The web is now essentially complete, although the spider may make a few alterations to the hub and, in some species, such as *Argiope*, a stabilimentum may be added.

The ease with which the spider moves on the web, which after all is a trap for arthropods, is amazing and it is difficult to understand how she avoids becoming trapped in it herself. It is noticeable that she always sits outwards, with her body kept clear of the sticky spirals, moving by grasping the dry lines in her tiny claws. Remember that web-builders have specially modified feet with an extra claw and opposing serrated hairs between which the silk thread is grasped (Fig. 2.6). Twisting her feet at an angle tensions the thread and holds her securely in position, while an oily covering on her legs prevents them from becoming attached to the sticky threads.

Having completed her web, the spider is now in a position to catch a meal to replace the protein and energy that she has used up in its construction. According to species, she will now either sit head downward at the centre of the web or else will retire to a nearby retreat constructed of silk, to wait for the arrival of prey. When in her retreat, the spider maintains contact with her web by touching the signal thread attached to the hub with her feet. As soon as a flying insect blunders into the web, she detects its frantic struggles and comes rushing out of her retreat and across the web towards the victim, tensions in the web's radii telling her its exact position. In fact, all of the information she requires concerning the size and position of the prey are communicated to her through her legs, since her eyesight is too poor to be of any assistance. The tiny vibrations set up by a small insect will send her rushing straight in to bite it and wrap it in silk, but the more powerful vibrations set up by a larger insect entail greater circumspection, in case the prey is a stinging wasp, capable of killing the spider given the chance. Small spiders may cut such a prey free of the web but mature specimens will tackle almost any prey, rushing in to deliver a bite at the first opportunity and then using the hind legs to rotate the prey while a mesh of fine silk from the spinnerets wraps it in a shroud. Once it is safely wrapped, the spider either carries it to the hub or, by following the signal thread, takes it back to the retreat to be eaten. Like many spiders, the orb-web-builders often masticate their prey using their chelicerae and maxillae to pulp the flesh into a more manageable state for digestion.

The spinning of such an orb web normally takes less than an hour, a remarkable achievement for a structure of such complexity, and many spiders construct a new web every night. For a new web, the existing foundation lines are utilised, the damaged threads usually being rolled up and eaten, an excellent example of recycling, for they consist of protein which the spider cannot afford to waste. The incredibly tough webs, made of yellow silk (Fig. 6.10), of the large *Nephila* spiders are strong enough to give a considerable amount of resistance to the advance of even as large a creature as a human being and consequently they are left in position for a fairly long time. Their huge occupants spend the day and night sitting in the centres of the webs, which have special garbage lines stretching from the hub to a labyrinth at the top of the web. Along this garbage line are strung all the sucked-out remains of prey, which occasionally includes small birds.

The feather-foot spiders of the family Uloboridae have independently evolved an orb web, although this is always horizontally arranged rather than vertically as in most Araneidae. Uloborid webs also contain dry and sticky silk and the spiders must depend solely upon these to subdue their prey for they lack poison glands. The web normally has a stabilimentum beneath which the spider hangs in an inverted position. The Uloboridae are mainly tropical in distribution and, in Britain, there are only two species, including the triangle spider, *Hyptiotes*, which is also found in the USA. These spiders are unusual in that they build a triangular web (Fig. 6.11), whose

Fig. 6.10. *Nephila senegalensis*. The web of strong yellow silk made by this large orb web spider hangs between the vegetation in an area of semi-desert in Kenya.

Fig. 6.11. Web of a *Hyptiotes*. The triangle spider forms a bridge between the anchor line and her web. When an insect strikes the web, the spider releases the slack silk, further entangling the prey.

construction is too complex to explain in detail but whose functioning is of great interest. The spider takes up a position at the apex of the triangle with her hind legs attached to a silken anchor on the twig behind her. Then she pulls on the bridge-line with her front legs until the whole web is tautly strung, leaving the slack looped over and held in her third pair of legs. In this position, her body now completes the bridge-line of the web as she hangs suspended in mid air. In this seemingly awkward position, she waits motionless until some insect flies into the web and adheres to the sticky threads. Instantly, *Hyptiotes* releases the slack and the web springs forward, pulling the spider with it. The trap may be sprung several times until the spider reaches the insect, which by now is hopelessly enmeshed. The victim is then wrapped in silk and transported back to the corner of the web, where further large quantities of silk are added before feeding commences, a process which can last a whole day.

The stick spiders of the genus *Miagrammopes*, from the USA, Africa and Australia, have gone even further than *Hyptiotes* in reducing their web to a single line only. This single line is usually just over a metre in length and is slung between two twigs. The central portion of the line, about half its length in fact, is then reinforced with a dense band of sticky silk. The spider then sits at one end of the line, with her back legs almost touching the twig to which it is attached, and draws it taut with a loop of slack held over her body in much the same way as *Hyptiotes*. The reinforced central area seems to act as an attractive alighting place for flying insects and, if one lands, the spider lets go the slack on the line, further entrapping the prey which is then dealt with in a manner similar to that of *Hyptiotes*.

WEB-CASTING SPIDERS With the exception of the reduced structures just described and one or two others, the web acts as a passive trap, the spider merely waiting patiently for the prey to enter it. The great diversity of kinds of web and their often great abundance in a particular habitat testifies to the efficiency of this method in ensuring a reliable and constant supply of food for the spider. A few web-builders, however, employ a more active method for catching prey, either by throwing the web over an insect, as if casting a fishing net, or by angling for insects with a sticky globule on the end of a line.

The best known exponents of web-throwing are the gladiator, ogre-faced or stick spiders of the genus *Dinopis*, which are mainly tropical but do penetrate into the USA. These strange spiders spend the daytime resting in undergrowth, where they resemble twigs or buds, but at night they become active and it is then that they construct their wonderful snare. Working on a small framework of dry silk, the spider lays down a mesh of extremely sticky and dense threads to form a net which is both strong and very elastic (Fig. 6.12). Hanging from four dry lines, she picks up the completed net in her four front legs and, in an inverted position, her legs drawn in close to her body, she waits for an insect to pass by. As soon as an insect comes close enough, the spider straightens out the four front legs way above its head, opening the net

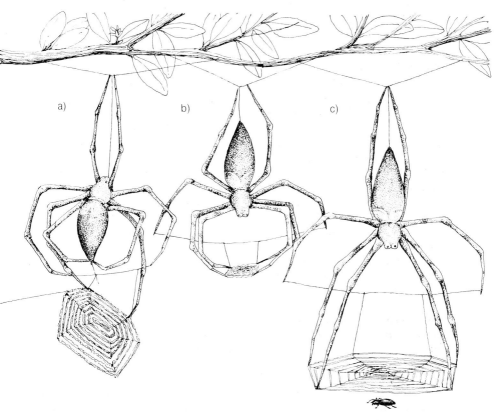

Fig. 6.12. Construction and use of the retiarius web of the net-throwing spider *Dinopis*. a) The spider constructs her net, holding it in her back legs. b) She then hangs waiting for prey to pass by underneath, the elastic net in its contracted state. c) As the prey passes underneath, the spider opens the net and spreads it over the insect.

out wide so that the insect flies in to its sticky mesh where it quickly becomes entangled. If the attempt is successful, the net is bundled up round the prey and it is then bitten and fed on through the mesh. Several attempts may be required before a capture is made but, even if the net becomes tattered, a new one will not be manufactured until the next night. A net which has escaped damage while catching a small victim will be used again but it is usually bundled up and eaten at daybreak. Sometimes, however, an undamaged net may be carefully stowed between nearby twigs or leaves and then carefully retrieved for further use the following evening.

BOLAS OR ANGLER SPIDERS Bolas spiders are found in various parts of the world, including much of the USA, and are certainly amongst the strangest of their kind, not only on account of their looks, for their fat, wrinkled bodies are adorned with horns and lumps, but because of their unique method of catching prey.

The American bolas spiders of the genus *Mastophora* are members of the Araneidae and they spend the day clinging to a leaf or branch where their hunched shape and muted colours make them difficult to spot. At dusk, each individual spider attaches a single horizontal silk line to the underside of a twig, then, hanging from this trapeze-line, she draws from her spinnerets a second line about 50 mm (2 in) long, at the free end of which she attaches a globule of very sticky gum about the size of a small bead. This is her fishing-line and this simple device is all that she requires to ensure an adequate supply of food.

Aroused by the same twilight which spurred *Mastophora* into action, plump moths now flutter quietly through the gathering darkness and sooner or later one of them will fly close to where the spider is sitting with her baited line. As the moth approaches, the spider seems to sense its coming and prepares herself for action. Precisely as the moth flies within range of the line, *Mastophora* swings it towards the approaching insect. If her aim is true, the sticky globule strikes the moth, which sticks firmly to it like a fly to a flypaper (Fig. 6.13). Larger moths flutter wildly in their efforts to escape but the

Fig. 6.13. A bolas spider using its 'fishing line'. a) As the moth approaches, the spider whirls the line like a bolas. b) With luck, the moth contacts the sticky droplet on the end and is trapped.

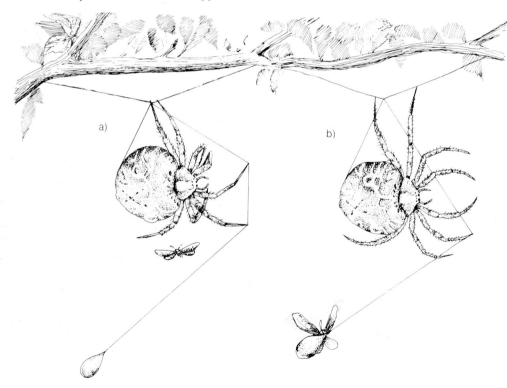

spider stands firm and draws it towards her until it is close enough for her to administer a paralysing bite with her fangs. Resistance quickly fades and the victim is wrapped in silk before being eaten.

It seems beyond the bounds of possibility that such a method of catching prey would fill the needs of a growing spider, since the likelihood of a moth passing within range would seem to be rather remote. It is, therefore, possible that the bolas spider ensures a regular supply of visitors by emitting a scent which attracts them to her. She normally uses only one line for about 30 minutes and then replaces it with another; this is probably necessary due to the drying out of the sticky globule and its consequent loss of stickiness.

The South African bolas spider, *Cladomelea akermani*, introduces variety on this theme by holding her line in her hind legs. Rather than just swinging this line at the moth once it is within range, she whirls it continuously for about 15 minutes in a horizontal plane. If her bout of assiduous whirling proves unproductive, she bites off the globule, eats it and replaces it with another.

Such a thrifty use of silk would seem to be the limit to which any spider could go and still manage to catch prey and yet the orchard spider, *Celaenia*, another Araneid, has taken the ultimate step and dispensed altogether with the use of silk. The orchard spider sits in full view on a branch, merely reaching out and grabbing any moth which comes in range with her spiny front legs. As with the bolas spiders, it is possible that the orchard spider uses an attractant scent to draw the moths towards her. *Arcys* (Plate 6.8) from Australia, although an Araneid, behaves like a crab spider, which it resembles, and ambushes its prey on flowers or leaves.

Plate 6.8. *Arcys lancearius*. This unusual Australian Araneid has given up its orb web and, instead, ambushes its prey in much the same manner as the crab spiders, which it closely resembles.

SPITTING SPIDERS Perhaps the prize for the most original way of capturing prey should go to the spitting spiders of the family Scytodidae, which includes the small black and yellow *Scytodes thoracica* found in Britain and the USA, where it lives mainly in human habitations. Although a few tropical species build small webs, most of these small spiders have no obvious means of catching prey, since they lack the speed and sharp sight of the hunting spiders. The key to their success lies in their ability to squirt a jet of gum from their chelicerae in the following way. With the potential victim a few millimetres distant, the spider raises its head and squirts two lines of gum over the insect's body (Fig. 6.14). The lines of gum, which fall in a zig-zag pattern produced by a rapid side to side oscillation of the chelicerae as it is discharged, pin the insect down. The spider then proceeds to administer the fatal bite, although, if a larger victim struggles excessively, *Scytodes* acts with more caution, biting it several times in the legs until its struggles cease. When the prey is dead, it is torn free of its sticky bonds before being consumed.

Fig. 6.14. The spitting spider, *Scytodes*. Once the prey is within range, the spider spits out two streams of sticky gum from special glands on its domed carapace. Simultaneous side-to-side movements of the head produce the zig-zag distribution of the threads which hold the fly firmly down.

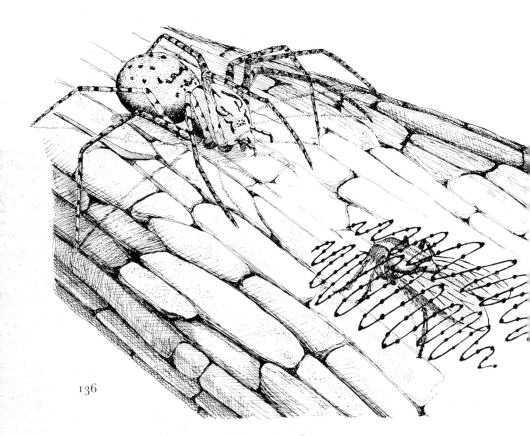

SOCIAL SPIDERS Spiders from a number of different families have taken up a social way of life, often with very large numbers of spiders sharing an enormous communal web (Fig. 6.15). In order for a group of spiders to live together in this way, some form of immediate recognition is necessary within the society, for the members are just as aggressive as their solitary cousins. Some clues as to how this social arrangement is made to work have come from studies on the social African funnel web spider, *Agelena consociata*. These revealed that recognition of members of the social group was a result of their production of typical vibrations when moving about in the web; a spider made to vibrate artificially was immediately attacked, although the attack stopped as soon as it made contact with its fellows, indicating that some chemical means of recognition also operates. Prey captured by members of the group is shared with any other spiders within the vicinity and, since young spiders remain within the web, this means that they can share food caught by more experienced adult spiders.

Social spiders from other families have much the same rules. The South African Theridiid species, *Anelosimus eximius*, forms colonies containing hundreds or even thousands of members of both sexes living harmoniously together in a light, transparent web which sprawls erratically over trees or bushes and may reach a metre across. The spiders move around freely within the web, feeding together in the interior of the web on insects caught around its periphery. The Eresid species of *Stegodyphus* from southern Asia and Africa construct enormous, fluffy, three-dimensional webs, which may envelop a whole tree and, in some parts of India, may join up to cloak the vegetation for several kilometres. Prey is normally confronted by a group of these spiders, who may quarrel initially over ownership but eventually a spirit of

Fig. 6.15. The communal araneid *Metepeira spinipes* from Mexico, with both males and females present, whose webs covered bushes and overhead telephone lines for several hundred metres along the side of a road.

co-operation will prevail and the food is taken to the central living quarters to be shared.

Commensal Spiders

Finally in this chapter, mention must be made of those spiders which make use of prey caught by other spiders, the commensal spiders. One such example is the Theridiid, *Argyrodes*, which typically lives within the enormous webs of the huge *Nephila* orb web spiders, where it is ignored by the owners on account of its small size. It is the small insects, which become trapped in these webs but are of no consequence to the *Nephila*, that are consumed by *Argyrodes*, who thereby helps its host by keeping the web clean and tidy.

Another commensal spider is *Uloborus ferokus*, which lives in the huge social webs of *Stegodyphus* in India. Both males and females are found within the web, along with egg-sacs and young spiders, so that the whole of this species' life cycle takes place in the host web. Not only does *Uloburus* make use of the prey caught by the web but it has been reported that the sticky web also protects its cocoons from the unwanted attentions of egg-parasites.

Chapter 7
Spider Defence Mechanisms

Spiders have to cope with not only natural enemies but also climatic and physical factors in their environment and it is the various ways in which they attempt to overcome these problems which will be discussed in this chapter.

The enemies of spiders are legion and, to increase the chances of surviving to perpetuate their kind, spiders have responded by evolving a number of survival strategies, prime amongst which is the avoidance of actually being found by a predator. This has been accomplished in two main ways, the first of which is to live concealed in a tube or burrow under the ground, with a well camouflaged door sealing the entrance. Predators initially have to locate the position of the burrow and then gain access to it, either by digging, as do the larger predators, such as coatimundi, or by crawling down inside the burrow, as do the predatory wasps. The second line of defence adopted by the spider lies in the resemblance of many of them either to the background on which they spend their lives, the bark of forest trees being a good example, or by mimicry of some inedible object within their environment, such as a twig or a dead leaf. There is another line of defence which should perhaps be mentioned—that of numbers. Spiders which live sheltered lives with no or few enemies, such as those which spend their lives in caves, have only a relatively small number of offspring as a high percentage of these survive to reproduce. Those spiders, however, which live exposed to all the dangers of life in an open meadow or a forest edge often have an excess of egg production to ensure that some at least of the baby spiders will survive to reproduce their kind. Whichever method of survival is employed, and many spiders have no obvious means of avoiding a heavy toll being taken of their population by predators, the numbers of each species remain remarkably constant over long periods, any large change in population density being caused mainly by what is perhaps the greatest single enemy of spiders, the weather. Drought, flooding or an exceptionally long and cold winter will drastically reduce numbers, although often only in the short term, for the weather will have a similar effect upon the spiders' predators, reducing their numbers and thereby giving the spiders a breathing space in which to breed and build up to their former numbers.

Fig. 7.1. A Malaysian mygalomorph sitting outside its burrow.

An Underground Existence

Many spiders lead a subterranean existence, but the obvious specialists in this way of life are the mygalomorph spiders, the majority of which live in burrows below ground (Fig. 7.1). The pre-eminent artisans within the mygalomorphs are the trapdoor spiders, which have acquired the skill of being able to construct a silken door to ensure privacy within their homes. A number of different types of burrows and doors of increasing complexity can be distinguished. The more simple types consist of a tube closed by a thick cork door neatly bevelled around the edges to fit snugly in the doorway (Fig. 7.2). Then there is the simple tube with a thin wafer door closing the entrance, while of the more complex types there is a burrow, closed at ground level by a thin door and having a second tunnel branching obliquely off the main tube, this branch tunnel also being closed at its entrance with a door. A number of even more complicated arrangements of doors and branched burrows are known, especially amongst the Australian trapdoor spiders, while the thick cork door gradually intergrades into the thin wafer door when examined on a world basis.

True trapdoor spiders have modifications for tunnelling, the most important of which is the *rastellum*, a series of strong spines on their chelicerae, which they use to dig into the ground. They use the rastellum to help them cut away the earth, which is moulded into little balls and then discarded outside of the burrow. A mixture of soil and saliva is then used to render the walls of the burrow with a waterproof coating and this is followed with a silken lining, which may or may not cover the whole burrow wall, depending upon the species. Immature spiders dig a small burrow which is

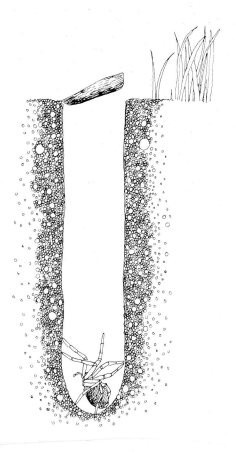

Fig. 7.2. Simple nest burrow of the trapdoor mygalomorph *Ummidia* from the USA, showing its thick cork door, which normally closes under its own weight.

gradually enlarged as they grow. Parts of the burrow are normally made sufficiently broad to permit the spider to turn around and, in this apparently secure environment, they live out their lives until overtaken by old age, since these species are naturally long-lived species, or until they are taken by one of the predators which can broach the apparently impregnable armour of their lairs.

The doors to the burrows are usually extremely inconspicuous, often flush with the ground and camouflaged with sticks, moss and leaves, and the most obvious indication of their presence may be an open burrow whose occupant has met its end. In this position, however, it is rather vulnerable to inundation by seasonal floodwater and burrows in situations where this is likely to occur on a regular basis, such as in parts of Australia, have turrets or palisades around the entrance to act as a barrage against water (Fig. 7.3). Despite its beautiful construction and perfect fit, the door to the burrow is its Achilles heel as far as the spider is concerned for, however well camouflaged it may be, its very presence allows those predators, well practised in its detection, to find the burrow and its occupant. Some trapdoor spiders cling to the underside of their doors if an enemy tries to gain entrance by prising it up, holding on with remarkable strength and tenacity against any upward pull on the door. The American species of *Ummidia* have, on their third pair of legs, a smooth process resembling a saddle, which often has a row of stiff spines around the edge. These press into the side of the burrow or the lip of the door, which is then gripped with the chelicerae and held tightly closed. Calculations have been made which show that another species, the Californian trapdoor spider, *Bothriocyrtum californicum*, can resist an upward pull of thirty-eight times its own weight. Many other trapdoor spiders do not use their chelicerae to grip the door but, instead, reverse their position and pull the door down firmly using the tarsal claws of the fourth pair of legs, which are hooked securely into the door's silk.

The most terrible predators of these spiders are probably the Pompiliid wasps mentioned earlier (p. 102) for they are capable of defeating and paralysing even the largest species, despite being in their own well prepared defensive positions. These formidable wasps are perhaps the ultimate in efficient predators from the insect world, well adapted for taking prey which

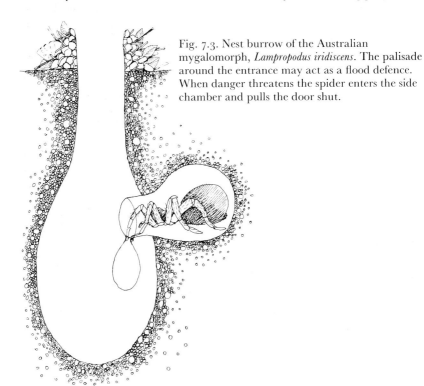

Fig. 7.3. Nest burrow of the Australian mygalomorph, *Lampropodus iridiscens*. The palisade around the entrance may act as a flood defence. When danger threatens the spider enters the side chamber and pulls the door shut.

is itself a rapacious killer. It is their finely tuned sensory apparatus and extremely rapid movements, coupled with their ability to curve their flexible abdomen in a complete circle inwards to administer a sting, while still grasping the victim in their legs or jaws, which makes them an almost impossible opponent for the spider to resist.

Hunting wasps which specialise in trapdoor spiders run restlessly over the ground with their antennae constantly quivering, easily detecting even the most highly camouflaged of burrow entrances. If the spider is not aware of its enemy's arrival, the wasp simply flips open the trapdoor and rushes into the spider's lair without the slightest hesitation at approaching so ferocious a predator in its own abode. Spiders which sense the wasp in advance may cling tenaciously onto the underside of the door, but this is to no avail as the wasp's powerful jaws just snip away at the silk curtain. The spider then usually panics and retreats down its burrow, inevitably to its doom, for its familiarity with its burrow endows it with no protection against the marauding wasp which then paralyses it with its sting. The wasp then either lays an egg on the spider or drags it away to a specially dug burrow of its own where it then lays an egg. Wherever the spider is, whether in its own home or in the wasp's burrow, it is then slowly eaten alive by the grub which hatches from the egg. In the former situation, the spider's fortress home now becomes its tomb and its building skills have failed it. Yet this is not really surprising, for insects are the most formidable of enemies and always seem capable of overcoming the most sophisticated of defence mechanisms, whether they be poisons evolved by plants, the camouflage adopted by others of their kind (and, of course, the spiders), the trapdoor spider in its supposedly impregnable home or man's insecticides, which become progressively less effective.

One of the stranger strategies employed by trapdoor spiders is exhibited by the weird *Cyclocosmia truncata*, a rare spider found in Georgia, Alabama and Tennessee. The round abdomen of this spider is chopped off short and furnished with a sort of leathery shield scored by a series of radiating grooves (Fig. 7.4). At one time it was thought that the spider sat head downwards in its burrow and blocked the entrance with this odd device, like a cork in a bottle but, since the entrance to the burrow is wider than the spider's abdomen, this cannot be the case. It is now known that *Cyclocosmia* covers the entrance with a normal hinged trapdoor, similar to that of other trapdoor spiders and of the wafer type. When, however, the spider is molested in any way it retreats to the bottom of its burrow, which narrows gradually as it deepens, and there presents its armoured shield to the intruder (Fig. 7.5). At this depth, the spider fits so perfectly and clings so tightly that it is impossible to pull it out without damage; to collect a specimen unharmed, it is necessary to dig the earth from round its body. This spider, therefore, has two lines of defence, for if the trapdoor is broached then it is further protected by its armoured abdomen. Less unusually built spiders, which have only the protection of a wafer-thin but well camouflaged doorway, depend some-

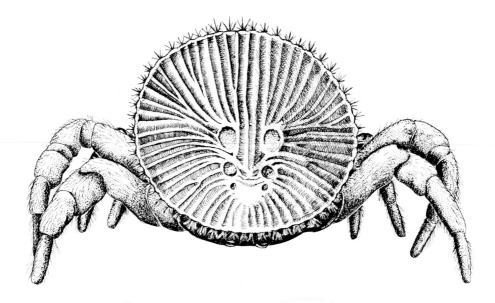

Fig. 7.4. The rear of the abdomen of the American mygalomorph, *Cyclocosmia truncata*, is covered in an armoured plate.

times upon deceiving any intruder by retreating into a side tunnel with its own separate doorway. In Australia, the wishbone spiders of the genus *Dekana* derive their name from the shape of their burrows, which are forked like a letter Y. The main shaft opens directly to the air at the surface while the secondary shaft opens out close to the main entrance but is capped with a collapsible escape hatch sprinkled with dirt and leaves (Fig. 7.6). If a predator enters through the main entrance, the wishbone spider charges straight out of the side entrance and makes good its escape.

Again in Australia, the striking black and white magpies, which are so characteristic of the local scene, have been watched feeding on trapdoor spiders, which were taken as they held their doors ajar in the early morning. The birds simply snipped off the spider's abdomen with their powerful beaks, leaving the rest of the spider wriggling on the ground in its death throes. The marsupial bandicoots spend the night foraging on the ground and they dig for a variety of foodstuffs, including trapdoor spiders, but, in Australia, the chief scourge of these spiders seems to be the centipedes and scorpions, which are able to penetrate the burrows and feed on the occupants. The huge Ctenizid, *Anidiops villosus*, of Western Australia has evolved an effective method of countering the attacks of these centipedes and scorpions. As well as having a camouflaged door at the surface entrance to the burrow, this spider also builds a collapsible sock halfway down the shaft.

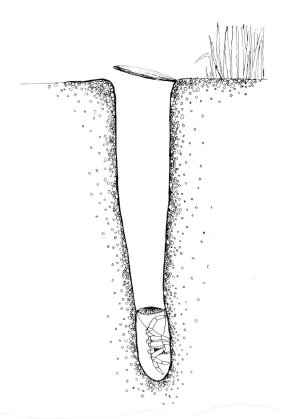

Fig. 7.5. *Cyclocosmia* in her burrow with the armoured plate fitting neatly across it and preventing attack from behind. USA.

Fig. 7.6. The brown wishbone spider, *Dekana*, in its burrow. The side entrance on the right is lightly covered with debris and, should a predator attack through the main entrance, the spider makes good its escape up the side burrow. Australia.

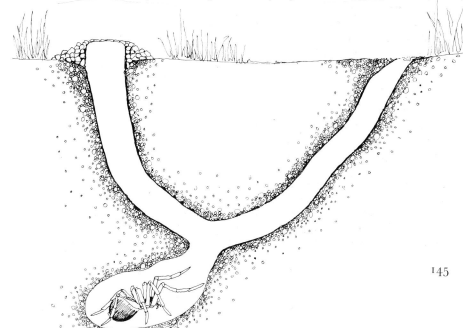

The spider often stashes its garbage, consisting of prey remains, around this sock, so that it forms a kind of flexible trash bag (Fig. 7.7). If threatened by a predator at the entrance, the spider retreats to the underside of the sock and pulls it down, the whole thing crumbling so that a pile of rubbish rains down on top of the spider, effectively concealing it from further investigation. In South Australia, the common pellet spider, *Stanwellia nebulosa*, builds a remarkably sophisticated and elaborate variation on this theme. This spider lines only the lower portion of its burrow with silk, leaving a loose collar about halfway up. On one side of this collar, the spider fixes the neck end of a pear-shaped pellet, which rests in a chamber dug into the side of the shaft, at least while the collar is in the open position. When frightened, the spider moves below the collar and pulls it downwards, which has the effect of bringing the pellet out of its chamber and into the burrow above the collar, effectively plugging it (Fig. 7.8). The thicker end of the pear-shaped pellet stays in the mouth of the chamber so that, when the spider pushes the collar open again, the weight of the thicker end acts as a counterweight pulling the pellet back into the chamber. To function perfectly, the pellet must be a perfect pear shape, a rare state of affairs for a natural pebble, so the spider manufactures its own by mixing together silk, saliva and mud and carefully moulding the plastic mixture into the required shape. The chamber into

Fig. 7.7. The twig-line burrow of the Australian species, *Anidiops villosus*. a) The spider, at the entrance to her burrow, testing a twig for vibrations produced by passing prey, with the sock half way down in the open position. b) The spider is now below the sock, which she has pulled down to provide a false bottom to the burrow, hiding her from the marauding centipede.

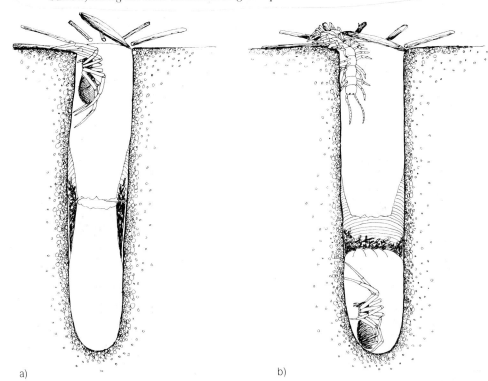

a)   b)

which the pellet fits must also be hewn out with some precision until everything is a perfect fit.

Not all spiders that construct burrows are mygalomorphs and a number of wolf spiders have taken to a subterranean existence, notably those of the genus *Lycosa*. The Australian *Lycosa stenni* is called the pebble spider because it stoppers the entrance to its burrow with a pebble seated neatly on a cushion of silk. A number of other Australian members of the same genus are called palisade spiders, each different species constructing its own particular kind of palisade around the entrance to its burrow. Some set up vertical rows of twigs, others lay them in a criss-cross fashion, one over the other, much as a log cabin is constructed, while the so far undescribed shuttlecock spider builds its palisade out of long, slim acacia leaves, which protrude several centimetres above the ground, to resemble a badminton shuttlecock. Each of these presumably helps to camouflage and provide a degree of physical protection for the spider's burrow.

Various species of *Lycosa* with burrowing habits are also found in Europe and the USA, although not in Britain. As with the trapdoor spiders, the burrows are dug using the chelicerae, although a rastellum is absent from the wolf spiders. Small packets of soil are tied together with silk and transported in the chelicerae to a disposal dump outside the burrow. The walls of the

Fig. 7.8. Burrow of the pellet spider, *Stanwellia nebulosa*. a) Here the collar is open and the counterbalanced pellet is in the side pocket. b) The spider hidden below the pellet which she has pulled out of its socket by hauling on the collar. Australia.

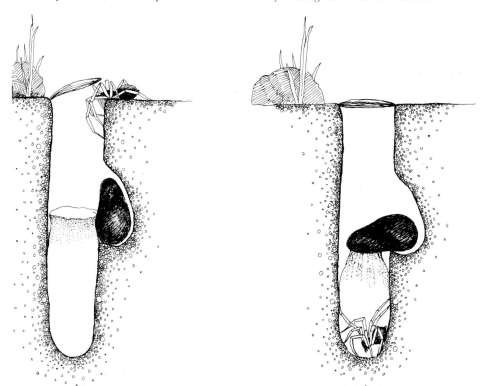

a)   b)

shaft are then covered in a silken blanket furnished with a webbing ladder which facilitates the spider's movements up and down the burrow. Some species cap the burrow with a turret, while the tiger wolf, *Lycosa aspersa*, builds a wall of moss and litter around the entrance to its burrow and surmounts this with a canopy of silk, leaving an entrance on one side. The silk roof is then decorated with lumps of soil, leaves, twigs and moss so that the entrance to the burrow becomes virtually undetectable.

A number of rather mottled spiders of the genus *Arctosa*, known in the USA as sand wolves, occur in that country and also in Europe, where *Arctosa perita* (Fig. 7.9) is quite common in Britain on coastal sand dunes and other similar habitats. The females are attractive spiders, with a pale body speckled liberally with black and brown markings and with dark rings on the legs. When sitting in the open on sand, these colours allow her to blend in perfectly with her surroundings and she remains completely invisible until she betrays her presence by moving. Generally, however, she spends much of her time inside a silk-lined burrow in the sand, lying in wait and springing out on any suitable passing insect. The burrow is basically Y-shaped; one of the branches leads to a dead end close to the surface, but the other branch is kept open on fine days, with the spider waiting at the entrance, although it is closed up during inclement weather. When danger threatens, she rapidly draws a silken curtain two-thirds of the way across the doorway, sealing up the gap in seconds with silk applied from her spinnerets. Such a beautifully camouflaged spider with an apparently secure retreat would be expected to be able to lead a reasonably secure existence but, as so often happens, her security is of no use against a Pompiliid wasp. The females of these wasps can detect the presence of the *Arctosa* burrow, even through its covering of sand,

Fig. 7.9. *Alopecosa accentutata*. This wolf spider blends in well with its background as it runs around on sand dunes or, in this instance, on fine limestone gravel in the Cotswold Hills in England.

using the taste sense on their antennae. On finding the entrance, a female wasp will bite a hole through the silk and rush inside without a moment's hesitation. In many cases, the spider has just sufficient time to run up the blind side branch, break through to the surface and make good her escape but, if the entrance happens to be open and the spider is taken by surprise, then her fate is sealed and she ends up as food for the wasp's larva.

Active Defence or Defence by Aggression

When caught out in the open or in the mouth of a burrow which cannot be closed, a number of spiders, particularly the larger mygalomorph trapdoor spiders and mygalomorph tarantulas, will react by adopting an aggressive posture (Plate 3.1), in which they raise their front legs and throw themselves back on their haunches, thus bringing the head upwards and exposing the formidable and capable-looking open fangs. A number of smaller and far more delicately built spiders, such as the notorious black widow and various small Australian spiders in particular, will react to persecution by actually biting the offender.

Many of the mygalomorph tarantulas are densely covered in a pelt of fine hairs (Plate 7.1) and, if persistently tormented, these species will lift up their abdomens and, by vibrating their hind legs, scrape free a puff of fine abdominal hairs. The mucous membranes of the eyes and nose of mammals, including man, are very sensitive to contact with these hairs, which induce severe watering of the eyes and an extremely unpleasant urtication, which may persist for some time and resembles the effects of similar hairs produced by some caterpillars. It has been shown that these spider hairs can penetrate human skin to a depth of 2 mm ($\frac{1}{16}$ in), aided by the many tiny hooks which each bears and which function as barbs. Any small mammals, such as coatimundi or racoon, which sniff closely at one of these spiders, will inevitably have its eyes within range of the puff of hairs, which must be extremely effective in giving the spider a few seconds during which to get away to safety. Spiders of this type from the USA normally have an area of these hairs on top of the abdomen and individuals who have had to make frequent use of them develop a bald spot which is replaced at the next moult with a fresh supply of hairs. The effect of these hairs is probably not just due to their physical structure but may also be magnified by the toxins which coat them. Some of them even incorporate the hairs into the silk of their retreats, bringing on severe symptoms of urtication in any animal which interferes with them, a habit which also has its parallel in the insect world, where various caterpillars incorporate their stinging hairs into their pupal cases. In neither case, however, are they any protection against predatory and parasitic insects. The Sydney funnel web spider, *Atrax robustus*, is dealt with in more detail in the next chapter on account of the severity of its bite in man, but it is worth mentioning here that the defence used by this spider is that of aggression and the females, when disturbed, have the unnerving

Plate 7.1. This tree-dwelling mygalomorph has a thick covering of hairs, which in some species can painfully irritate the human skin. Trinidad.

habit of exuding a globule of poison from the tip of their fangs, which is clearly visible and certainly very off-putting to humans.

One final defensive ploy of a particular kind is seen in some of the larger South American mygalomorphs, which come out at night and sit on the trunks of trees, waiting for suitable prey to come their way. When disturbed, these slow-moving giants calmly turn their rear end towards the troublesome object and squirt at it a clear liquid from the anus, a habit also adopted by the giant stink-bugs, *Pachylis*, of the family Coreidae, which are found in the same part of the world. The liquid produced by *Pachylis* is foul-smelling, foul-tasting and has irritant properties and these features may well be true of the liquid produced by these spiders.

A form of passive defence employed by all spiders is the life-line, which is constantly paid out behind the spider wherever it goes. This is of special importance to those spiders which live above ground for, if threatened in any way, they can let go and swing out of harm's way on their life-line.

Camouflage

Under this heading, it is intended to present the use by spiders of two different but related forms of protective device. In the first place there is camouflage (alternatively called *crypsis* or *cryptic colouration*), which applies to the colours and patterns of the spider itself and, secondly, there is camouflage with regard to the coverings applied by the spiders to its home or egg-sacs to render them less conspicuous, often by the use of naturally occurring materials, such as bark, moss and leaves. Before looking at this subject in relation to the spiders, however, the evolution of cryptic colouration in the animal kingdom as a whole is worth considering, for it is widely met with in birds, reptiles, amphibians, fish and a host of invertebrates, especially the insects and spiders. With the exception of the very largest carnivores, such as the great cats, the majority of animals fall victim to others, even though they themselves may be formidable predators upon other animals. The frog, for example, which feeds upon insects, spiders and other small invertebrates is itself the prey of larger animals, such as snakes and water birds, which in their turn may fall victim to foxes and birds of prey. Cryptic colouration not only renders an animal less visible to its predators but also enables it to approach its prey or indeed, encourages the prey to approach it.

Camouflage of Spiders

The majority of spiders spend at least some of their time in the open, where they are visible to potential predators. Some species, such as the crab spiders, lead lives which, by their very nature, expose them to enormous possible danger, particularly from birds, which are voracious predators, with sharp eyesight allied to a degree of intelligence far higher than that found in the invertebrates. The likelihood of being spotted by a bird will be appreciably reduced if the spider can blend well into its surroundings and so the gradual evolution of crypsis gives a considerable survival advantage.

CRYPSIS Certain animals have carried this evolution to a fine state of perfection, not only by having the ability to match the colour and pattern of their immediate background but also by being able to change colour and pattern as they move from one background to another. The most familiar exponent of this behaviour must be the chamaeleon (a lizard), but the ability to change colour is also a characteristic of certain spiders.

Unless there is some accompanying change in the behaviour of the animal, crypsis is of little value. Its advantages will, for example, be immediately lost if the cryptic predator moves for it will instantly become visible not only to its proposed victim but also to any larger predator in the vicinity to which it may well fall victim itself. Instead, the camouflaged hunter either pursues its prey with great stealth, moving very slowly like the chamaeleon, or else it remains motionless, waiting patiently for a meal to come within range. The role played by the two types of camouflage in the lives of spiders may be considered by looking at some specific examples.

Flower Spiders The crab spiders of the family Thomisidae are the prime examples of spiders which lead mainly sedentary lives, waiting in ambush for the arrival of insect prey, and it is this habit which gives them the alternative name of ambushing spiders. A number of well known Thomisids lurk in ambush in flowers and, in these spiders, their colours match either part or all of the flower. Similar cryptic colouration has evolved in the flower bugs and in the flower mantids, both of which are mainly sedentary predators. Since the flowers involved are insect-pollinated, it is simply a matter of these flower-dwelling predators sitting and waiting for the arrival of their victim.

Almost certainly, the best known of the flower-dwelling crab spiders is *Misumena vatia*, which is widely distributed on both sides of the Atlantic, while, in the USA, the closely related genera *Misumenops* and *Misumenoides* are frequently met with and lead similar lives. *Misumena vatia* is most often white in colour, with darker markings on the cephalothorax and, sometimes, with varying amounts of pale red along the sides of the abdomen (Fig. 7.10). There is also a bright yellow form (Plate 6.3), which is much less often seen and the spider can, in fact, change from one colour form to the other in a few days. The spider normally selects a flower which matches the colour of its own body and over 80% of individual spiders are found on such flowers. In Britain, *Misumena* is particularly common on the ox-eye daisy, *Chrysanthemum leucanthemum*, which has a large yellow central disc surrounded by conspicuous white ray florets. The spiders on these flowers are almost invariably white, despite the large yellow centre, and they sit beautifully concealed on the ray florets, only occasionally straying onto the yellow area. Various investigators have established that many different kinds of insects will avoid flowers in which a dark object is present, so matching the colour (or at least the shade of grey, since most animals see in black, white and grey) of the flower gives the crab spider a distinct advantage. Not only will it not be obvious to insects landing on the flower but also its chances of being eaten by birds, whose sharp eyes would soon pick out a spider of a contrasting colour sitting out in such an exposed position, are reduced. This does not always hold true, however, for the yellow form of *Misumena* may be found in both blue and pink flowers, where, at least to human beings, it can be very easily spotted; nevertheless it may be present in the same flower for at least 2 weeks without being eaten while at the same time securing a plentiful supply of insect food. In this and any situation, the spider derives a measure of protection by remaining perfectly still, for even if its colour contrasts with that of the flower, it might well resemble a normally contrasting flower centre; if it is disturbed, however, it will often sidle slowly over the edge of the flower and hide underneath until it is safe to emerge again. Despite their almost perfect camouflage, it is interesting to report that, as usual, the

Fig. 7.10. *Misumena vatia*. The more common white form of this species, a female, is engaged in consuming an Empid fly, itself a predator. Europe and USA.

Plate 7.2. *Thomisus onustus*. This attractive crab spider blends in well with the pink flowers upon which it is normally found. Europe.

hunting wasps seem to have no problems at all in finding these spiders and the nests of some of the American mud dauber wasps are often crammed full of *Misumena* almost to the exclusion of any other spiders.

The very beautiful *Thomisus onustus* (Plate 7.2), a crab spider which is rare in Britain but found widely in Europe, lives in much the same manner as *Misumena*. It may either be a very pale yellow or pink, the latter form being the normal one in Britain, where it is mainly associated with pink flowers, such as heathers and spotted orchids. The rather triangular abdomen is somewhat lumpy and this, combined with its pink colouration, makes it even harder to spot than *Misumena*. One way of finding both of these species, and, indeed, any crab spider anywhere in the world, is to look for insects which appear to be sitting strangely still while feeding on a flower. If below the flower there is a pile of the carcases of earlier meals, dropped there by the spider, then the chances are that the rather still insect has the crab spider's fangs sunk into the back of its neck.

Bark-Dwelling Spiders The Australian crab spider, *Stephanopsis altifrons*, has a number of spiny and knobbly outgrowths on its body and legs which enable it to blend perfectly into the rough bark of the various species of trees which it inhabits (Plate 7.3). This is but one of a large number of spiders belonging to several different families which spend their whole day sitting in full view on the bark of trees; of these, the largest number of species and some of the best camouflaged examples live in tropical rain forests. Many members of the family Hersiliidae exhibit this habit and, in common with all spiders which live on a flat surface like bark, the body tends to be flattened to

Plate 7.3. *Stephanopis altifrons*. A cryptic crab spider on tree bark in Australia.

reduce the amount of shadow it casts; this could otherwise betray its position on the trunk of the tree. *Tama* (Plate 7.4) and *Hersilia* are both long-legged hunters belonging to the Hersiliidae and there are also a number of Thomisids and Sparassids with similar habits. The most impressive of all is

Plate 7.4. *Tama* sp. This is one of the so-called two-tailed spiders of the family Hersiliidae, which live upon the bark of trees against which they are very well camouflaged. Sri Lanka.

Fig. 7.11. *Pandercetes gracilis.* A female lichen spider from Australia showing the tufts of hairs on her legs which resemble lichen, giving her her name and camouflaging her beautifully against the lichen-covered bark on which she lives.

undoubtedly *Pandercetes gracilis,* the lichen spider (Fig. 7.11), a Sparassid found in the tropical rain forests of Australia and New Guinea. This fairly large spider sits head downwards on a tree trunk with its two front pairs of legs facing forwards, while the third pair lie out at the sides and the fourth pair point backwards. The whole body is covered in short hairs, which give the spider a matt finish, resembling the lichens on the bark, which are also closely matched by the mottled colouration of the cephalothorax and abdomen. To complete the effect, the legs are liberally furnished with flattened tufts of hairs which eliminate any shadows which unadorned legs would cast on the trunk. These Sparassids and the bark-dwelling Thomisids spend the whole day in one place, thereby avoiding any risk of betraying their position by moving, but some of the tropical jumping spiders do hunt actively over the bark, their mottled colours blending in well with it and in at least one species, which lives in rain forest in Sri Lanka (Fig. 7.12), the legs are lined with rows of hairs similar to those of *Pandercetes*. If they sense that their presence has been detected, these little hunters react by freezing instantly and flattening themselves against the bark, whereupon they apparently disappear in front of the startled gaze of any predator.

A number of orb web spiders do not build a silken retreat in which to hide away but, like the spiders above, spend the day in full view, either on the

Fig. 7.12. An incredibly camouflaged jumping spider on a tree trunk in rain forest in Sri Lanka.

flattish bark of the main trunk or on smaller branches or twigs. Queen among these spiders is *Herennia ornatissima* (Fig. 7.13) and its relatives from the Malayan and Australasian regions. The female's flattened whitish abdomen, patterned with red, has fluted edges and is pressed closely into her

Fig. 7.13. *Herennia ornatissima*. This female Araneid comes from Malaysia and she improves her camouflage by sitting in a silken cup on white-lichen-covered bark. The tiny male can be seen above her and to the right.

silken nest, which is usually made on trees with a covering of whitish lichen into which she blends extremely well. Sometimes her egg-sac, camouflaged with white silk into which she has stuck flakes of lichen-covered bark, can be discerned just beside her. Both *Hersilia* (Plate 7.5) and *Pandercetes* females can often be found sitting on guard above their white egg-sacs, which are affixed closely to the bark and are well camouflaged with bits of bark chipped off by the spider using her chelicerae. In the Shimba Hills in Kenya, a beautiful Argiopid, possibly a species of *Clitaetra*, encloses her egg-sacs in rather elongated swathes of silk and sets them in the centre of her web, which is

Plate 7.5. *Hersilia* sp. This is a female spider sitting on a tree trunk above her egg-sacs which she has camouflaged with small pieces of flaking bark. Kenya.

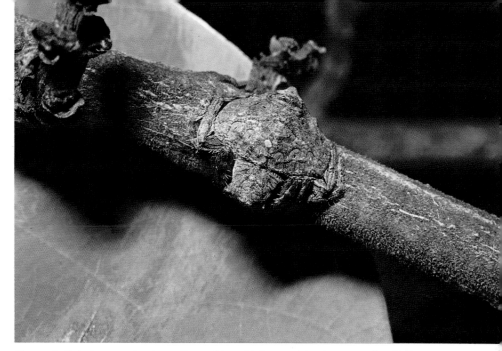

Plate 7.6. *Dolophones* sp. An Australian spider which resembles the protrusion (left) where a twig has broken off a larger twig.

placed a few millimetres or so above the bark of a tree. The spider herself is very pretty, silvery white with red and black marks on the abdomen, and she spends the day sitting with her legs closely applied over the silk covering her egg-sacs. As she always seems to build her web on a tree which is liberally covered in white lichen, she is, like *Herennia*, extremely well concealed in her rather vulnerable position.

Selection of a suitable resting place is also very important in spiders which seek to blend in by resembling a natural protrusion on the surface of a tree. The *Dolophones* twig spiders in Australia hunch down on their fairly slim legs, the knobbly body completely spanning a twig and resembling a protruding lump of bark (Plate 7.6). *Poltys* lives in the same habitat but has a much taller and more angular abdomen, surmounted by two sharply conical humps. It assumes a strange position with the front two pairs of legs held over the face with just the eyes left peeping out, while the two rear pairs are pressed closely against the sides of the abdomen. It chooses rather larger branches than *Dolophones*, a couple of centimetres or more in diameter, and in this strange posture it resembles the jagged end of a small broken-off branch.

Britain and the northern states of the USA lack the outstanding examples of bark-dwelling spiders outlined above, but a number of smaller species have adopted this habit and, despite their insignificant stature, are of some interest. The most familiar of these in Britain is the Linyphiid, *Drapetisca socialis*, whose counterpart in the USA is *Drapetisca alteranda*, and both of them are associated with the bark of deciduous trees, beech being the main choice of the British species. When not actively hunting, they lie close to the bark and, despite their rather rotund shape, they are surprisingly difficult to pick out in the dim light below the beech canopy.

MIMICRY It is clear from certain of the preceding examples, that not only do some spiders have colours and patterns which match their surroundings, but a number of them have also changed their shape as well to match that of inanimate objects around them. There are in fact many spiders which resemble dead leaves, buds, twigs or bird droppings and a selection of these will now be considered.

Leaf Mimics A large number of the world's species of *Araneus* have brown abdomens patterned with a rough leaf outline (Fig. 7.14), which helps to

Fig. 7.14. *Araneus ceropegius*. The leaf-shaped marking on the abdomen of this species is typical of many members of the genus *Araneus*. Europe.

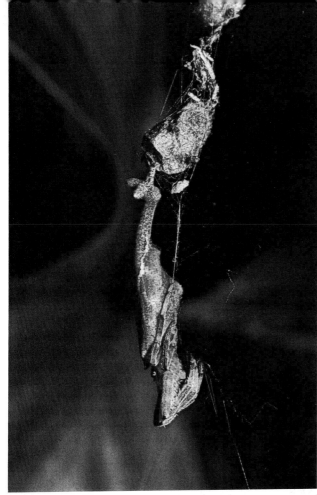

Fig. 7.15. Arachnura sp. The scorpion spider from New Guinea hangs from its web in such a way that it resembles a dead leaf, the projection on its abdomen representing the leaf stalk.

improve their camouflage as they spend the day curled up in a real dead leaf. Going further than this, *Araneus redii* habitually sits exposed on dead, brown seed-heads of thistles, knapweeds and similar plants, where it resembles a dry, brown fruit. In Australia and New Guinea, there are the strange elongated scorpion-tailed spiders of the genus *Arachnura*, whose slender abdomens sometimes bear a number of blunt projections at the tips. The female hangs a string of her brown egg-sacs down the web and then hangs head down below them, looking like a dead leaf with the tip of her abdomen resembling the leaf stem where it broke away from the twig (Fig. 7.15).

A number of other spiders also mimic leaves but in different ways. The African Salticid, *Portia schultzi*, is the most extraordinary creature, particularly the male, which has a mass of golden hair on the palps, two brown 'ear tufts' on top of the head, a large number of long spines along the legs and a very slender brown abdomen (Plate 7.7). Even when moving in its characteristic jerky manner this little spider looks amazingly like a small, wrinkled, dead leaf being blown along by an intermittent breeze and, when stationary, with its legs pulled into its sides, the resemblance is complete. Some far more sedentary spiders employ a similar form of mimicry. In the

Plate 7.7. *Portia schultzi*. A Kenyan jumping spider, a male in this instance, which resembles a crinkled dead leaf.

tropics, for example, there are many crab spiders with flattened lumpy abdomens which sit with their legs drawn into their bodies on some foliage leaf, where they closely resemble a leaf which has died and dried up and fallen onto the living leaf below (Plate 7.8). Various members of the Araneid genus *Micrathena* from the Americas bear spikes and lumps on their wrinkled abdomens and, sitting in the centre of their webs, look for all the world like a dead leaf which has lodged in the web on its way to the ground below (Plate 2.2).

Plate 7.8. A Trinidadian crab spider which resembles a wrinkled dead leaf lying upon a living leaf.

Spiders which are green and, therefore, are camouflaged against or mimic living vegetation, are far less common than the previous examples which mimic dead parts of plants, perhaps because birds seek the bulk of their food on the living rather than the dead parts of plants. A number of lynx spiders, particularly several beautiful species of *Peucetia* (Plate 7.9), habitually hunt

Plate 7.9. *Peucetia viridans*. The male of this American lynx spider is well camouflaged against the green, stinging 'mala mujer' leaf on which he is sitting.

over green leaves, which they closely match in colour, and the lovely European Sparassid, *Micrommata virescens*, has similar habits. These spiders often sit in full view on their leaves but, as long as they remain motionless, they are extremely hard to spot.

Twig, Stick and Stem Mimics Dinopids are sometimes called stick spiders because of their resemblance to these inedible objects but other spiders also look like twigs, sticks and grass or rush stems. As in many of the spiders discussed above, mimicry of these inanimate objects requires a modification not only in structure and colour but also in behaviour. Some of the best and most familiar examples of this are found in the Tetragnathidae, the grass spiders. *Tetragnatha extensa*, whose bizarre courtship was described earlier (p. 76), is commonly found in grass and reeds around water in its European range. Its body is very elongated, usually yellowish in colour with various markings, and the legs are long and slender, except for the third pair, which are much shorter than the others. In its typical attitude when out of its

Fig. 7.16. *Tetragnatha extensa*. This typical pose of members of this genus, when they are not in their web, has earned them the common name of grass spiders.

web, it sits head downwards along the stem of a grass or rush (Fig. 7.16), holding on to it with its short third pair of legs, with the first two pairs stretched out forwards and the fourth pair out backwards. It is very difficult to distinguish when in this position while, on the occasions when it adopts this posture in its web, it resembles a small stick or piece of grass which has lodged in the silk. Crab spiders of the genus *Tibellus* adopt a similar posture for, unlike the squat, fat majority of this family, they have long narrow bodies. Their customary pose is head downwards along a grass blade or stem and, from this position, they pounce upon any insects which pass their way.

Bird-Dropping Mimics Mimicry of bird-droppings by the caterpillars of various moths is a well known phenomenon and, even in Britain, several adult moths mimic these inedible objects, which are certainly not included in the menu of predatory animals. In the tropics, however, butterflies and several types of fly are very attracted to bird-droppings for the salts which they contain and butterflies may sip avidly from them for long periods.

Fig. 7.17. *Phrynarachne decipiens*. A crab spider from New Guinea which sits on a leaf where its resemblance to a bird-dropping is enhanced by the 'splashes' of white silk around it.

There is obviously both an aggressive and a protective advantage to be gained by a tropical spider in resembling a bird-dropping for, if its mimicry is successful, a source of food will come to it to be taken at the spider's leisure and it will be effectively protected from its own predators while it sits in full view waiting for its prey to arrive. The phenomenon is known in a number of spider families but the most celebrated species is probably the crab spider, *Phrynarachne decipiens* (Fig. 7.17), of Malaysia, and similar species in New Guinea. The whitish, wrinkled spider itself looks like the excrement from a bird but the effect is enhanced because it sits on a small·mat of white silk resembling the white part of the dropping which spreads out as it hits the leaf. In Trinidad occurs a small species of *Micrathena* which spends the day on a leaf, with its legs hunched around its rather long, lumpy body, resembling a more elongated dropping and, in Kenya, there is an Araneid (Fig. 7.18) which seems to have forsaken its web and instead sits on a leaf, where its shiny blob of a body resembles a particularly wet, fresh, and to insects particularly

Fig. 7.18. A spider from Kenya belonging to the family Araneidae, which closely resembles a fresh wet bird-dropping.

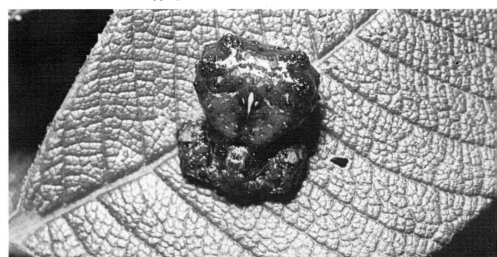

attractive, dropping. (The photograph used in Fig. 7.18 is of a spider which the photographer mistook for a bird dropping while he was photographing another subject near to it. So good was its mimicry that he actually took steps to avoid touching what he thought was a fresh dropping.)

Ant and Wasp Mimics Mimicry of ants is found amongst spiders the world over and has been developed to the peak of perfection in certain tropical Clubionids. Ants are generally rejected by most birds and many other predatory creatures which are quite happy to take a wide variety of other insects. There are obvious advantages to resembling an unpalatable insect although, interestingly enough, some ants are the prey of the spiders that mimic them, an example of an ant-eating spider being the Salticid *Cosmophasis* from Kenya (Plate 7.10). It is, in fact, to the Salticidae that the most familiar ant mimics belong and a number of physical and behavioural modifications have been necessary to perfect their disguise. Their bodies and legs tend to be long and slender and, in some species, the cephalothorax and abdomen have a very constricted pedicel, just like the waist of an ant. Spiders which cannot achieve a true waist often do so by deception, pale bands across the body at strategic points doing the job almost as well as the real thing. Just as important as physical resemblance to the ant models are changes in the spider's behaviour, especially in its mode of locomotion. Ants are continually on the move in their environment in a quest for food for the colony and the spider therefore behaves in the same manner; the constantly vibrating antennae of the ant are copied by the spider waving its front pair of legs, the other three pairs thereby corresponding to the six legs characteristic of insects. Many ant-mimicking spiders also move their abdomens in the same way as ants and move with an ant-like gait and it takes very close scrutiny and a practised eye to spot the deception in some instances. Some ant mimics actually run with their models or live within the ants' nest while others merely occur in the same habitat as the ants where they lead a solitary existence.

In the tropics, the resemblance between ant model and spider mimic is

Plate 7.10. *Cosmophasis* sp. A male jumping spider from Kenya, which mimics the ants on which it feeds; here the spider is on the right and its ant prey on the left.

Plate 7.11. *Cephalotes* sp. A genus of ants which is found in the rain forests of South America.

often faithful to an extraordinary degree. In Trinidad the Clubionid spider, *Myrmecium* (Plate 3.5), is almost indistinguishable from species of *Megalomyrmex* ants while, in Peru, one of the most amazing of all examples of ant mimicry by spiders occurs. In the Peruvian rain forest, ants of the genus *Cephalotes* are often very common. These are large black ants, very heavily armoured with broad square heads, with a heavy spine projecting on either side at the top, and a surprisingly small, rounded abdomen stuck on the end of a distinct pedicel (Plate 7.11). These formidable ants are closely mimicked by the spider *Aphantochilus* (Plate 7.12), which resembles the model in every respect, even down to the projecting spines on the head. Certain species of spider have gone so far as to mimic one species of ant when they are adult and a different species in their immature stages.

Perhaps as interesting as the ant mimics is the amazing Salticid, *Orsima formica*, which does not, as its name suggests, mimic an ant but instead mimics one of the vicious-stinged Mutillid wasps, but in reverse. The spinnerets at the tip of the spider's waisted abdomen are exceptionally long for a Salticid, thereby resembling the antennae and jaws of a wasp. As it

Plate 7.12. *Aphantochilus* sp. A spider which very closely mimics ants of the genus *Cephalotes*. Here a female spider is sitting over her egg-sac. South America.

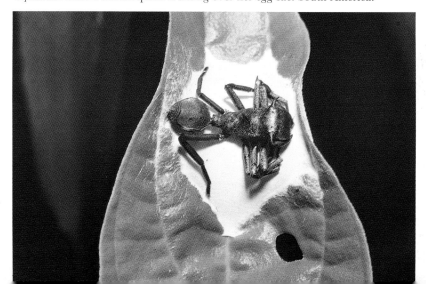

moves, the spider waves its abdomen around, copying the movement made by the head of the wasp as it searches the leaves in the rain forest. Periodically the tip of the abdomen is depressed onto the surface of a leaf in an action similar to that made by a wasp feeding. The rear pair of legs are much darker in colour than the others and this, combined with the long, dark spinnerets and the bright colour of the abdomen complete the idea of there being a pseudo-head at the rear. This disguise is so effective that, when watching this spider running restlessly over a leaf in the manner typical of its model, it becomes difficult at times to remember which end is which.

Camouflage of Egg-Sacs, Webs and Lairs

Apart from the odd passing reference, little has been said so far about camouflage of egg-sacs, webs and lairs, but this is carried out in different ways by a number of spiders; for instance, many tropical orb web spiders camouflage their webs in some way. Some pale-coloured species distribute their similarly coloured egg-sacs in a circle around the hub of the web; they then sit in the centre, both spider and egg-sacs looking like the shiny wings of wrapped prey or other similar objects caught in the web (Fig. 7.19). The *Cyclosa* spiders are small and elongated, usually with conical lumps on the end of the abdomen. The centre of their web, which is often built close to a tree trunk, is bisected by a dense stabilimentum consisting of the remains of past meals bound together with silk to form a bundle; mature females later add their egg-sacs to the string. This stabilimentum is divided into upper and lower portions with a gap between into which the body of the spider neatly fits. The top of the spider's abdomen is usually silver or off-white to match the silk and, in this position, the edible spider is almost impossible to

Fig. 7.19. It would be difficult for a predator to distinguish this female Araneid in the centre of her web from the ring of egg-sacs around her. Peru.

distinguish amongst the mass of inedible silk and debris (Fig. 7.20). In much
the same way, a Kenyan *Cyclosa* packs its rubbish into a mass at the centre of
the web and extending slightly upwards from it. Around the hub, she spins
an irregular band of white silk and then she sits inconspicuously at the

Fig. 7.20. *Cyclosa* sp. Sitting in the centre of her web, this spider is hardly
distinguishable from the remains of prey strung out above and below. Kenya.

Plate 7.13. *Cyclosa* sp. This female spider from Kenya is sitting amongst the
remains of her insect prey, where she is almost indistinguishable from them.

bottom of the mass of brown debris, where she is hard to see amongst the numerous remains of dead insects (Plate 7.13).

In Australia, the leaf rolling spider, *Phonognatha*, rolls up a dried leaf and, after binding it together with silk into the shape of a tube, hangs it at the centre of the web. Snug inside this retreat, the spider communicates with its web by sitting with its front tarsi in constant contact with it, in much the same way that other spiders sit in their retreats outside the web. In Kenya, a brown and black lynx spider encloses its mass of eggs in the cradle of a dead leaf suspended in mid-air between a number of silk lines. She sits there guarding her eggs, perfectly matching the dead leaf and virtually invisible except by close inspection, the mid-air position making her inaccessible to predators (Plate 7.14).

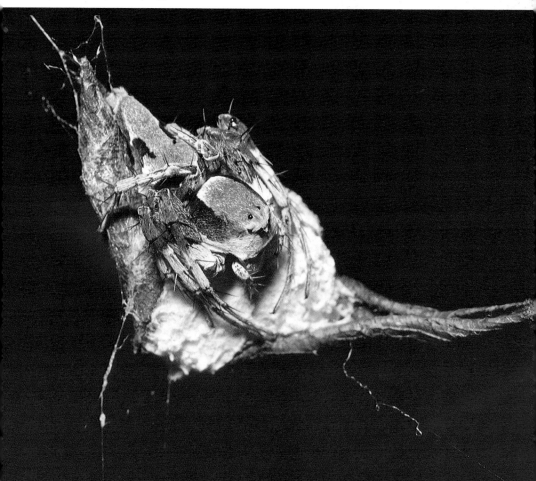

Plate 7.14. A very cryptic lynx spider, guarding her eggs which she has placed in a rolled leaf suspended in her web. Kenya.

Other Defence Mechanisms

Finally, there are some points which do not fit into the previous categories but do, however, relate to spider defence mechanisms. The incorporation into the web of a stabilimentum consisting of zig-zag bands of shining white silk (Fig. 7.21) is common within the Araneid genus *Argiope*. For many years, it was thought that its function was to strengthen the web or else to help conceal the spider, which often sits head downwards at the centre of the stabilimentum. Some neat experiments in the USA have established that

Fig. 7.21. *Argiope* sp. The zig-zag of silk which form the stabilimentum typical of some orb web spiders show up well in the web of this Malaysian spider.

their function is quite the reverse, for they actually advertise the presence of the web to birds, which frequently fly into webs lacking stabilimenta because these webs are so difficult to see. The construction of the web uses a considerable amount of the spider's protein supply and, if it is subsequently destroyed by a bird accidentally flying through it, then its constituent protein is lost to the spider, for spiders recycle protein by eating old or damaged webs. Since the silk of these orb web spiders is covered in liberal amounts of sticky glue, this will also be of advantage to the birds, allowing them to avoid the web on seeing the stabilimentum and thus preventing them becoming covered in sticky silk.

It has already been made clear that the most frequently used method of defence in orb web spiders is simply to hide away in a retreat constructed to one side of the web. If, however, it is disturbed when in the centre of its web, the orb web spider may react in a number of ways. Most frequently it makes a headlong dash for the security of the retreat but some spiders seldom seem to do this and, instead, simply let go of the web and fall to the ground on the end of their life-line, where they lie with their legs pulled in to their sides. As many of these spiders are mottled in greys and browns, they become virtually invisible amongst the detritus on the ground below the web. The third and most unusual method of defence involves the rapid vibration of the web as the spider sits at its centre. The oscillations are at such a high frequency that the occupant of the web becomes a blur and, presumably, under these conditions, it would be nigh on impossible for a bird hovering in front of the spider to pick it off the web with its beak. The huge *Nephila* spiders also employ this tactic and this can be alarming even to a human being as the giant long-legged spider vibrates into a blur in the centre of its enormous yellow web.

Chapter 8
Spiders and Man

Generally speaking, man's relationship with spiders is a remarkably neutral one and, apart from the very small number of poisonous species, spiders have little apparent effect on the day-to-day life of mankind. The drastic alterations to the environment of man's farming and industrial activities are, on the other hand, having an increasingly harmful effect on many animals and plants and, consequently, spiders, which require a particular type of natural habitat in which to live and prosper.

Attitudes and Uses

In many countries of the world, the general attitude towards spiders is favourable and members of a considerable number of different cultures consider it unlucky to kill a spider, whether by accident or by design. This tradition may have arisen as a result of the feeling that spiders must be beneficial to man as they are responsible for the destruction of such large numbers of insects. This is something of an oversimplification of the way in which spiders influence insect populations and it is based on the assumption that nearly all insects are pests, which, of course, is very far from the truth. The most significant controlling agents, which prevent insect numbers reaching alarming proportions, are insects themselves, especially parasitic wasps and flies. Because spiders are unselective about which insects they catch, it means that beneficial insects are just as likely to fall prey to them as pests. Since in any given area, the majority of spiders are likely to be small, they will catch small prey and, since many of the parasitic insects are also small, they are very vulnerable to being caught. The insects that these parasites affect, however, are often much larger and can only be taken by larger spiders, which occur at much lower densities. The result, therefore, is that spiders are more likely to take parasites than they are to take the parasites' pest hosts. On this basis, ideas that man has had of using spiders as agents for biological control do not appear as straightforward as one would think and, in the past, such attempts have had only a limited success and then only in rather artificial situations, e.g. using large crab spiders to control bed-bugs in buildings.

Although many people, especially in the West, feel a high degree of revulsion towards spiders and may in fact be frightened of them, in some areas of the world they may actively encourage spiders to enter their homes or may even take them in themselves. The houses in villages in certain areas of the Sierras in the state of Michoacan, in Mexico, suffer invasions by huge swarms of flies which congregate in them during the rainy season. To rid themselves of this nuisance, the villagers employ a novel form of biological control. In the mountains near the villages, many of the trees are covered with the massed webs of the communal cribellate spider, *Mallos gregalis*, whose local name is the mosquero. The webs of these spiders may clothe a whole tree, so the locals just cut off a handy-sized branch, which is taken home and hung from the ceiling. The swarming flies land on the sticky threads and become ensnared, whereupon they are removed and eaten by the web's occupants.

Such a practical use of spiders to control an insect pest, which in addition to being a nuisance, may also spread disease, is admirable but alas rather rare. Much more frequently, spiders have been used in an effort to control human diseases, but in a far less practical and effective manner. In Europe, from early times, spiders have been used as charms to keep disease at bay and both their bodies and their silk were prescribed by the medical practitioners of the day, by no means all of them doctors, to be swallowed by the unfortunate patient as remedies for gout, leprosy, jaundice, constipation, malaria and a multitude of other diseases. The more unlucky patients had to swallow the whole spider, alive and kicking, but other remedies called for dead spiders, spiders rolled up into pills or spiders ground up and made into ointments to be rubbed into the skin or brewed into potions to be drunk. There is, of course, not a shred of evidence to suggest that the trust in these remedies was anything but totally misplaced, but it took a long time for faith in this type of medicine to die completely, if indeed it has done so, especially in more isolated rural communities. One use of spiders, seemingly more effective and which may possibly survive today, is the application of their webs to a recent wound, the mesh of fine silk helping to staunch the flow of blood in a purely mechanical, if somewhat unhygienic, way.

Although the bodies of spiders themselves can have had little practical benefit to mankind, except perhaps as a valuable source of protein for certain primitive peoples, the strong, flexible silk they produce has been put to a variety of uses. Until relatively recently, spider silk was used in the reticules of a variety of optical devices, such as gunsights, where its unrivalled strength, considering its diameter, and its capacity for resisting variations in climatic conditions unscathed made it particularly suitable for this task. The multiple fibres of life-line silk, separated into individual threads, were used. Obtaining the silk is simply a matter of reeling it directly off the spinnerets of the living spiders, which are remarkably co-operative in this respect. Spider silk is still used in a number of applications but, in many cases, it has been superseded by materials which are easier and more accurate to work with.

A less successful attempt has been made to use spider silk in the production of textiles. Many people have dreamed of spider silk competing with the product obtained so effectively from the silkworm, the larva of a moth. Experience has established, however, that production of sufficient quantities of silk from spiders is far more complicated and expensive than it is from silkworms, whose silk is of a better quality, being thicker and more lustrous. The spiders which have been used most often in experimental work are the huge species of *Nephila*, whose silk is particularly thick and strong. One worker in the USA was surprised to find how simple it was to reel silk from the living spider and was able to obtain as much as 140 m (150 yd) from a single spider, which spun continuously for $1\frac{1}{4}$ hours. Nevertheless, even at this prodigious rate, the quantity produced was less than half that obtainable from a silkworm and, on this basis, it has been calculated that, to make a dress of average size, no less than 5000 of these enormous spiders would be required.

Primitive peoples the world over have always tended to use any naturally occurring objects or products in their surroundings to maximum effect, so it is not surprising to find that, in some places, the webs of spider, which are so abundant and easily obtainable, have been put to various practical uses. The aborigines of Northern Queensland show considerable ingenuity in their use of spider silk for fishing. A slim twig is inserted into the web of a *Nephila* and skilfully woven to and fro until the coarse threads are twisted into a line about 300 mm (12 in) in length. The unfortunate spider is then mashed up and smeared on the frayed ends of this line, the unused portions of the creature being tossed into the river, where shoals of small fish are immediately attracted to them. The silken lure is then towed across the water, attracting small fishes which rise up to nibble at the tasty morsels attached to it, whereupon the strands of silk become entangled in the fishes' teeth. The wriggling fishes are then pulled out of the water as another contribution to an aborigine meal.

The strong, flexible silk from *Nephila* is used for the same purpose by the natives of Papua but in a very different, although no less ingenious, way. The enormous webs of these spiders are abundant in the forest and are a readily available source of silk. Long bamboo poles are bent over into a loop and are erected where the webs occur most densely in the forest. A frame of this shape is particularly suitable for the spider, which obligingly spins its web across it, thereby constructing an instant fishing net, which is dipped into the river, any fish caught being thrown onto the bank. In another method of construction, a hoop is twisted through a large number of natural webs until several layers of silk are interwoven in a strong and durable mesh, which can then be used several times and requires the minimum of repair.

Poisonous Spiders

In Britain, the unthinking panic engendered instantly in many people by the mere sight of a spider is difficult to understand for, luckily, Britain has no spiders capable of harming a human being and only a handful of species big enough to be able to pierce human skin with their fangs. *Dysdera crocata* can certainly do so with its woodlouse-armour-piercing fangs, but the result is not serious, and the garden spider, *Araneus diadematus*, and house spiders of the genus *Tegenaria* have all been implicated in the biting of human beings, but again without effect. One rather surprising example of spiders biting man happened near Birmingham, when workers on a sewage farm reported being bitten by the tiny Linyphiid, *Leptorhoptrum robustum*, which made its home in large numbers in the clinker of the sewage filter beds. The bites caused a certain amount of irritation and swelling and, in some instances, the men had to leave work for a while to obtain first aid treatment. It is extremely surprising that so tiny a spider is capable of inflicting a painful bite on a human being but luckily this was an isolated and fairly trivial case.

The situation in most of the rest of the world is very different and a number of extremely toxic spiders are known. Female spiders of the genus *Latrodectus*, the notorious widow spiders, for example, have one of the most virulent of animal poisons on a weight for weight basis. *Latrodectus* of one species or another are almost cosmopolitan but the largest numbers of serious bites to human beings are reported from the USA, with lesser numbers from Europe and Australia. The citizens of Australia have to contend not just with poisonous spiders for they also have numerous poisonous snakes, jellyfish and even molluscs.

Generally speaking, the case against poisonous spiders has been greatly overstated in the popular press and, in the USA, the chances of dying from the bite of a widow spider is about the same as that of being struck by lightning. The most famous of these spiders is the southern black widow, *Latrodectus mactans* (Plate 8.1), a shiny black rather rotund spider with a characteristic red hourglass mark on the underside of the abdomen. Four other species of widow spiders also inhabit the USA, all of them being shy, sedentary spiders, which shun the light and retreat immediately when disturbed. Only the females are dangerous, but they are not at all aggressive and make no attempt to bite, even after extreme forms of provocation, but problems do arise, however, because of their habits of living in close proximity to man. The spiders may find their way into clothing or shoes, they may live amongst the logs in a woodpile or they may be found around the lids of dustbins or even around the seats of outdoor privies. In these kinds of situation, it is inevitable that, on the odd occasion, the unfortunate spider is going to be pressed against someone's bare skin and, under this kind of duress, the natural reaction of any animal is to bite in self defence.

When a bite does take place the effects are often serious, both in animals and in man. Within minutes of the skin being punctured, extreme pain develops around the site of the wound and this rapidly builds up to a maximum intensity in about 30 minutes. The intensity of the pain is reported as being 'almost insupportable' and this is one of the most notable symptoms of *latrodectism*, the name given to this condition. A number of other alarming symptoms develop as the powerful neurotoxic poison begins to affect the nervous system. The patient often feels nausea and may vomit; feelings of faintness and dizziness develop, accompanied by an increase in salivation, watering of the eyes and profuse sweating. Speech may be affected, breathing becomes difficult and the jaw muscles go into spasms which distort the face into a pain-racked grimace. Muscles all over the body may go rigid, especially those in the belly region, which may pull tight as a board, leading some doctors to the incorrect diagnosis of appendicitis or an ulcer. In the

Plate 8.1. *Latrodectus mactans.* The female black widow spider in her web built close to the ground in rough pasture in Mexico.

past, this has led to unnecessary operations and at least some of the deaths from spider bites in the USA and Europe have been caused by needless surgery rather than by the bite itself. In severe cases of poisoning, the patient may eventually become prostrate and die, very young children and old people being most at risk. In the past, death occurred in less than 4% of all bites, but nowadays an antitoxin is injected, which has a rapid and miraculous effect. The greatest puzzle, perhaps, is why this small spider, which has a large and very efficient web for prey capture, should possess a poison so potent that it is capable of killing an animal which is many thousands of times heavier than itself. The poison has, in fact, been calculated to be around fifteen times more potent than rattlesnake venom, one of the more powerful snake toxins.

All of the species of *Loxosceles* in the USA are also thought to be capable of administering an unpleasant bite, but with very different effects. The best known is *Loxosceles reclusa*, which has acquired a number of common names, the more appropriate of which are the brown recluse and the violin spider, the last name occasioned by the violin-shaped mark on the cephalothorax. Like the widow spiders, *Loxosceles* is often to be found around human habitations and at least five deaths have been reported from their bites in the USA. The toxins in the bite kill the cells surrounding the puncture, producing a black, gangrenous spot. Often the skin proceeds to peel away from the area around the wound, exposing the underlying tissues and, in extreme cases, an area 150 mm (6 in) across can be severely affected and, since the wounds are slow to heal, they can leave a very unpleasant scar.

As already mentioned, Australia has more than its fair share of toxic animals and numbered among them is the Sydney funnel web spider, *Atrax robustus*, a mygalomorph which, in recent years, has been the subject of more press coverage and has received more notoriety than any other species of spider. It has gained the reputation of being extremely aggressive, but this is probably just the normal reaction of any of the larger mygalomorphs in defence of their homes. Following a bite from this spider, symptoms develop rapidly, starting with immediate severe pain around the site of the puncture followed by a numbness in the same area. Feelings of nausea are followed often by vomiting, the patient begins to sweat heavily and then collapses. The lungs then become blocked with fluid and breathing becomes difficult. This results in the victim turning blue as he becomes starved of oxygen; he may often froth at the mouth. Unbearable cramps develop with severe pains in the arms, legs and abdomen. If not treated, the patient may become delirious, go into convulsions and eventually fall into a coma which may lead to death. Until recently, this was the almost inevitable course of events and children were particularly susceptible and sometimes died, but an antivenene has now been developed which quickly alleviates the symptoms and should eliminate the problem almost completely in the future. Australia has several other species of venomous spiders, including *Latrodectus mactans* and, to make matters worse, two Loxoscelids have been introduced by man.

The bite of a number of spiders in European countries other than Britain may cause unpleasant symptoms but these are very rarely, if ever, fatal. Strangely enough, even the bites of the huge mygalomorphs of tropical regions are rarely serious, the damage mainly being confined to the actual wound produced by their large fangs, although some smaller species are poisonous to a degree. In some parts of South America, however, wandering Ctenids of the genus *Phoneutria* sometimes make their way into people's homes where their bites have been known to be fatal to young children.

It is possible that there are species of poisonous spiders with very unpleasant effects as yet undetected, and, indeed, it is a spider which is suspected to be the cause of bites which, in Australia, result in a severe necrosis which eats right down to the bone. To put it in its correct perspective, however, the chance of a spider bite prematurely terminating one's life or causing severe illness is exceedingly remote and it would be as ridiculous to worry about the possibility of it happening as it would be to worry about being struck by lightning or having a tree fall on one's head.

Man's Effects on Spiders

The activities of man obviously can play a decisive role in the success or otherwise of most living organisms, including the spiders. Any species, for example, which is specialised for life in marshes and cannot survive in drier habitats will become locally extinct if a marsh is drained for agricultural purposes. On the other hand, spiders such as the Linyphiids occur in very large numbers in grassland, which is often a result of man's agricultural activity, but would not achieve such an abundance in the woodland which would more naturally occupy the site. Generally speaking, as with most other organisms, the effects of man on spiders are largely detrimental and the destruction of whole habitats, such as the species-rich tropical rain forests, threatens the survival of numerous spider species as well as all the other inhabitants and, in the final equation, man himself. Even when at first glance what man has done seems less drastic, the local floral and fauna may suffer adversely. In Australia, comparable surveys have been made of naturally occurring open woodlands, effectively fenced off from sheep and cattle, and of similar neighbouring land which was heavily grazed by both animals. Trapdoor spiders which were abundant in the fenced off areas were totally absent under the pounding hooves of the domestic stock, which by their trampling and erosion were rapidly destroying not only the rich local flora and fauna but the whole of the environment in which they were allowed to roam.

In the final analysis, however, spiders and their insect prey are far better equipped for survival in the long term than man himself and, whatever the shape or form of man's future follies, it is certain that spiders will still be laying traps for flies long after man has finally disappeared from the earth.

Appendix: Spider Families

Sub-order MESOTHELAE (primitive, segmented spiders)

Family   Liphistiidae

Sub-order ORTHOGNATHA (the mygalomorph spiders)

Family		Family	
Ctenizidae			Atypidae
Antrodiaetidae			Theraphosidae
Actinopodidae			Pycnothelidae
Migidae			Paratropidae
Dipluridae			Barychelidae
Mecicobothriidae			

Sub-order LABIDOGNATHA (the true spiders)

Ecribellate Spiders

Family		Family	
Dysderidae			Symphytognathidae
Oonopidae			Hadrotarsidae
Gradungulidae			Nesticidae
Caponiidae			Araneidae
Leptonetidae			Theridiosomatidae
Telemidae			Tetragnathidae
Scytodidae			Archaeidae
Loxoscelidae			Mimetidae
Sicariidae			Agelenidae
Diguetidae			Hahniidae
Plectreuridae			Pisauridae
Ochyroceratidae			Lycosidae
Pholcidae			Toxopidae
Zodariidae			Oxyopidae
Palpimanidae			Senoculidae
Hersiliidae			Ctenidae
Urocteidae			Gnaphosidae
Theridiidae			Clubionidae
Linyphiidae			Prodidomidae

Family Platoridae
        Homalonychidae
        Sparassidae (Heteropodidae)
        Selenopidae

Cribellate Spiders

Family Hypochilidae
        Hickmaniidae
        Filistatidae
        Acanthoctenidae
        Zoropsidae
        Oecobiidae
        Eresidae

Family Amaurobioididae
        Thomisidae
        Salticidae
        Ammoxenidae

Family Tengellidae
        Dictynidae
        Psechridae
        Amaurobiidae
        Uloboridae
        Dinopidae

Glossary

Alveolus The cavity in which lies the cymbium *q.v.*

Book lung A chamber, connected with the atmosphere, which the spider uses for breathing.

Calamistrum A row of hairs on the back legs of certain spiders used to comb out silk produced by the cribellum *q.v.*

Carapace The hard shield covering the top of the cephalothorax.

Cephalothorax The fused head and thorax of spiders.

Chelicerae The name given to the jaws of spiders.

Cribellum A plate through which a special kind of silk is produced in certain spiders.

Crypsis or **cryptic colouration** Where the spider's colour and pattern allow it to merge in with its background, another name for camouflage.

Cymbium Part of the tarsus on the male palp used to pick up sperm and transfer it to the female.

Ecdysis Another name for moulting during which the old exoskeleton is shed and replaced by a new one from underneath.

Embolus A stiff spur on the cymbium *q.v.*, through which opens the spermophore *q.v.*

End foot One of the many tiny hairs into which the hairs on the scopula *q.v.* are subdivided.

Epigyne A structure on the underside of the female's abdomen; it is associated with special sacs which receive sperm from the male.

Fang The piercing part of the spider jaw, through which runs the duct which delivers the poison via a small hole at its tip.

Hackled band A special combed-out, fluffy silk produced by certain spiders.

Labidognath The true spiders whose jaws strike from side to side.

Labium A plate which forms the back of the spider's mouth.

Maxillae A pair of accessory jaws used to break up the food.

Mimicry Where a spider copies the shape of another animal or some inanimate object such as a stick.

Mygalomorphs The more primitive spiders whose jaws strike forwards and down.

Palps The second pair of appendages attached to the side of the spider's head and used for sensory purposes. In the male, the terminal segment is modified for putting sperm into the female.

Pedicel The narrow waist which connects the cephalothorax *q.v.* and abdomen of the spider.

Pheromone A chemical produced by spiders to attract members of the opposite sex and maybe, in some spiders, to attract prey.

Rastellum A row of teeth on the chelicerae of some mygalomorph spiders used while digging the burrow.

Retina The layer of light-sensitive cells in the back of the eye.

Scopula A dense brush of hairs on the foot which allows the spiders that have them to grip onto smooth surfaces.

Sexual dimorphism Where there is a marked difference between the male and female spider to the extent that they may not be recognised as belonging to the same species.

Slit organs Sensory organs on the exoskeleton which detect stress.

Spermatheca A sac in the female spider's abdomen in which sperm from the male is stored.

Spermophore A blind-ended coiled tube contained in an inflatable bulb in the cymbium *q.v.*

Spinneret A structure on the hind end of the abdomen through which silk is extruded.

Spiracle The opening of the trachea onto the body surface.

Stabilimentum A special band of silk placed across the centre of the web of certain spiders.

Sternum The plate of cuticle which forms the underside of the cephalo-thorax *q.v.*

Tarantula Correctly ascribed to wolf spiders of the genus *Lycosa* from Europe but, in the USA, is the name given to the mygalomorph spiders while, in Australia, it is often the name given to the huntsman spiders.

Tarsal organs Small openings on the legs associated with chemoreception.

Trachea A tube, leading from the atmosphere into the spider, which is used for breathing.

Trichobothria 'Touch at a distance' receptors found on certain leg segments.

Urtication Literally being stung, as by a nettle, but applies in this instance to the effect produced by the hairs of certain mygalomorph spiders.

Guide to Further Reading

Bristowe, W.S. (1958) *The World of Spiders* Revised 1971. Collins, London.
This is one of the books in the New Naturalist Series and deals exclusively with the British spider fauna. It is very easy to read and includes many of Bristowe's own observations on the lives of British spiders.

Foelix, R.F. (19) *Biology of Spiders* Harvard University Press, Cambridge, Massachussetts.
Translated from the original German text, this book goes into considerable detail of the structure and physiology of spiders and is clearly aimed at the biologist rather than the layman.

Gertsch, W.J. (1979) *American Spiders* Van Nostrand Reinhold, New York, USA.
A parallel to Bristowe's book for the American spider fauna, it includes descriptions of representative members of most of the American spider families and includes at the end a list of species common to the USA and Europe.

Locket, G.H., Millidge, A.F. & Merrett, P. (1981) *British Spiders* Vols 1 & 2 combined. Reprint. Ray Society, London.
Locket, G.H., Millidge, A.F. & Merrett, P. (1974) *British Spiders* Vol. 3. Ray Society, London.
For those readers who would like to attempt to identify the British spiders, there are these volumes, produced by the Johnson Reprint Corporation. They are not easy to use since much of the identification requires the use of a good microscope, but they do provide information on the distribution of all of the British species.

Main, B.Y. (1976) *Australian Spiders* Collins, Sidney, New South Wales.
Again this does for the Australian spiders what Bristowe and Gertsch do for the British and American spiders respectively. The book is very easy to read and is extremely informative.

Index

Numbers in *italics* refer to black and white illustrations.
Numbers in **bold** refer to colour plates.